Become an Effective
Condo Board Member

Become an Effective Condo Board Member

Sandra Rosen

Writer's Showcase presented by *Writer's Digest*

San Jose New York Lincoln Shanghai

Become an Effective Condo Board Member

Published by Writer's Showcase presented by *Writer's Digest* an imprint of iUniverse.com, Inc.

For information address:
iUniverse.com, Inc.
620 North 48th Street
Suite 201
Lincoln, NE 68504-3467
www.iuniverse.com

ISBN: 0-595-09593-3

Printed in the United States of America

Reviews of Sandra Rosen's Course

First of all, the course in terms of content could not be better. All of the information well presented and of interest to anyone starting out on an Association Board of Directors or for those with some BOD time under their belts. I was gratified to find that many of the suggestions and directions you provided were things we were already doing but, as always, I found some things I hadn't even thought about. I was happy to see that a little humor made its way into those classroom sessions. It would have been fun to be a part of those sessions, I think.

I have copied the entire course on diskette for other members of the Board. I now hope, of course, that they will open the files and "take the course." It will make the job easier for the newcomers and will help me have a more cohesive Board with everybody singing from the same page in the song book. I think what you are doing here, Sandy, is a great benefit for all of us involved in Association Boards and an incredible bargain at the price. I hope it has been beneficial for you as well and will become even more so.

Keep up the good work and thank you.

Vince Compagno
President
Allenmore Ridge Condominium Association
Tacoma, Washington

I found your course very helpful and would highly recommend it to all existing and new board members.
Donna S. Gray, Minnesota

I must tell you that in the sixty or so days since your course I have shared information on at least three topics that were vexing us. I'd say your course is well worth the "price of admission."
N. Gail Weinrich
Illinois

When I first received class info, I was unsure exactly how the class was going to turn out. I was definitely surprised to find out how valuable the information is that I have received. I have also gained invaluable knowledge from this class.
Thank you for this class.
Ben Schreiber, President
Hidden Woods Condo Association, Inc.

This course is absolutely an excellent guide to Association living. It is exceptionally well organized, concise. practical and applicable to all phases and concerns of Association living. It is an excellent guide and resource for novice Board members to experienced Board members and has become mandatory reading criteria for our Association and Board members. I am a member of a small condo Association in North Truro Mass. Our basic problem was that most of the Association members were not aware of policy and procedures that govern Association living. This class has been a great asset to the understanding of policy and prodder as they affect decision making by board members and Association members. Sincerely,
Cheryl Lee CT.

Contents

About the Author

Author Profile

Sandy has been involved with property management since 1976. Specializing in the management of large communities of 1097 unit apartment complex and a planned urban development of 2300 units consisting of 15 individual Condo and Townhome communities and open space including single family homes association with numerous amenities in New Jersey.

I bring to the course my experience working with board members, owners/investors, and of being a professional association manager. Since 1981 I had been an active member of the Community Association Institute (CAI) where she instructed other professionals in the field. It is my goal that this course will help Board members become knowledgeable and confident in their Board positions.

I share my knowledge and experience with Board members, owners and potential unit owners in the hope that individuals will have a better understanding of the condominium concept and the communities will run more effectively and positively affecting the quality of life within those communities. Since developing and then teaching this class I feel very strongly that there are two books every condominium Board should own, one is the "Robert's rules of order" dealing with proper protocol for meetings and the other is "Become an effective Condo Board member."

The Homeowner Association

In order to be an effective board member you must first have an understanding of the documents of your community. Yes, you can rely on the management agent but you wouldn't be taking this class if you didn't want to be more confident, more knowledgeable and more effective as an officer. Let's begin with some discussion about the governing documents.

Ok, let's talk about what I call the Bible of a community, the governing documents. The (POS) or PUBLIC OFFERING STATEMENT which is given to new/perspective owners and contain all the governing documents. While laws my vary from state to state most states will require the developer to file three basic documents to be included in the POS: The declaration, the bylaws and individual unit deeds of ownership. The documents everywhere deal with the following:

1. Definition of the individual units and the common areas.
2. The percentage of ownership interest in the common and limited common areas.
3. The creation of the association and an outline of its purpose and administrative procedures.
4. Maintenance and contractual responsibilities.
5. Management agent requirements.
6. The initial operating budget.

7. Insurance requirements.
8. Rules and regulations.
9. How the transfer will occur from developer control to the home-owner control association.
10. The declaration or master deed as it is sometimes called, is the most important document relating to the community. It is the constitutional law of the association.

The declaration outlines the owners responsibilities to the association and the associations responsibilities to the owners. It defines all physical elements of the community and defines the methods of determining each unit owners share of common areas and assessment of common charges. The declaration outlines the common areas, limited common areas and unit boundaries as well as the requirements for the responsibility for maintenance.

Let me take a minute to clarify common areas or elements versus limited common elements. Common areas or common elements is the property within the community that is owned jointly by all unit owners and the cost to maintain is shared equally by all owners. That includes land and structures or portions of structures not otherwise described as belonging to one individual unit owner. Limited common elements is property that is part of the condominium's common area but reserved for the exclusive use of a particular unit owner, i.e. a patio or balcony.

The declaration establishes the administrative framework for the association. The bylaws provide the guidelines for governing the association, now stay with me.. I know it sounds a bit confusing. The declaration creates a board and dictates the number of members on that board and the bylaws spell out the method of electing the officers, and their duties.

The use restrictions are usually found in the bylaws.

It is essential that you know your documents well if you are a member of a board of directors. Do yourself a favor and find that *public offering statement* and leave it in the bathroom so you will find the time to read it. The documents are essential reading. If you have questions about your term of office, removing an officer(God forbid), election procedures, quorums, definitions of common property, insurance requirements for the common elements, formats for meeting agendas, how many meetings a board must have each year, protocol for annual meetings, distribution of notices for meetings, community budget approvals, fining for non compliance of rules, duties of board members. These are all things that are outlined and defined for you in the documents. You get these answers not just by calling the manager or asking the association lawyer during a meeting but by reading it for yourself. If you do not have the documents pertaining to your community get them immediately! If you are a board member call the management agent and have them send you one yesterday. If you are not on the board put your request in writing and forward that to the managing agent and they will direct you on how to get a copy. You also want any additional amendments or addendum's to the existing documents. Including any additional rules and regulations that may have been approved after the first set of documents were printed.

The success of a community including its appreciation of property values relies heavily on the rules, regulations and restrictions that govern residents conduct. The bylaws and house rules and regulations give specific guidelines for living. Many residents refer to the rules as "the gestapo tactics" but that's only when it relates to something they did or want to do and not if they have a problem with what a neighbor did or wants to do. You know what I mean don't you?

Now, there are two kinds of restrictions-*use restrictions* and *architectural restrictions*. Use restrictions pertains to encroaching on the rights of other unit owners and architectural restrictions are designed to protect the integrity of the original architecture and enhance property value.

The Governing Documents

The purpose of every organization of condominium unit owners is the same, to *encourage cooperation and to deal with all facets of the working condominium community*. This formal organization acts as a small government to settle differences of opinion among residents, collect and allocate funds to operate the community, maintain common areas and make all those decision that are vital to the unit owners.

Each and every owner belongs to the association and therefore is responsible for the economic and social success of the condominium community. Unfortunately, the role of the association often is not explained to the buyer by the real estate agent or developer sales representatives even though many potential problems could be avoided if it were.

The condominium association usually does not hold title to any property. However, it does serve as the vehicle for making decisions that affect property owned by all its members. Its responsibilities typically include:

(1) providing common services to and repair and maintenance of the common areas.
(2) protecting the unit owners' investments.
(3) establishing and collecting assessments to pay common expenses and establish reserves.
(4) enforcing the rules and regulations of the association.
(5) helping members live together and share common facilities.

These responsibilities and the ways in which they are to be fulfilled are set forth in a series of governing documents specifically designed for condominium ownership.

In the beginning, the developer holds the title to a plot of land that is recorded as an estate covered by only a deed, or a single deed estate. The law then approves the request of the developer to commit this land to the condominium form of ownership. In effect, the developer sets aside the land for the purpose of building a condominium and creating a condominium association to run it. It is the developer and not the people who someday will own a unit there, who establishes the condominium association.

The single deed estate is committed to the condominium plan when certain legal documents are recorded with the appropriate local government office. The number and kinds of documents the developer is required to prepare vary from state to state. **Most states, however, require the developer to file three basic documents-the** declaration, the bylaws, and the individual unit deed. These documents define who owns what in the condominium and outline the association's administrative procedures. Although not always required by state law, two additional documents-the articles of incorporation and the house rules and regulations also govern the condominium. Certain states also require that certain other documents be recorded with the primary governing documents.

The Declaration

The declaration, the master deed, the plan of condominium ownership, or the declaration of conditions, covenants, and restrictions (CC&Rs)is the most important legal document related to a condominium. It commits the land to condominium use, creates the condominium association, describes all of the physical elements that make up the condominium development, and defines the method for determining each unit owner's share of common areas. The declaration tells the unit owner what he or she is going to own and outlines their responsibilities to the association and the association's responsibilities to the owner. In effect, it is the constitutional law of the condominium association.

Because of the importance of the declaration, the conscientious developer should prepares it with the aid of project architects, landscapers, an insurance agent, a professional management agent, and an attorney. Since state laws governing condominium development vary, the content of a declaration written in one state may differ from the content of a declaration written in a neighboring state. In addition to complying with applicable state statutes, declarations also must fit the specific needs of each condominium development. As a result, one document may be 100 pages long while another may be only thirty pages long.

Even a well-prepared declaration may at times require an amendment. Therefore, procedures for amending the declaration should be incorporated into the document itself. The most common amendment request is in regards to the percentage of votes needed to pass specific items and most documents still require 75% of the membership to vote and that is for some crucial issues. Ironically amending of a declaration usually requires approval of a large percentage of voters often as much as 100%. So the association begins the long process of lowering that requirement. In reality most communities feel lucky to have a 25% turnout to vote. In view of the fact that amendment of the declaration may be very difficult, the developer should limit the document to only those provisions that are absolutely necessary. A well-written declaration should establish a strong association without imposing undue restrictions on the unit owners. If it does the members should amend it only after careful consideration. In addition, the association must confer with legal counsel prior to amending the declaration to assure that any proposed changes are not in conflict with state laws governing condominiums.

The condominium plat, a diagram of the total condominium area, is usually filed as an addendum to the declaration. It generally includes a survey map of the surface of the land, a metes and bounds description of the parcel of land, and floor plans of all buildings showing common areas and the individual condominium units. The plat is especially useful in locating the property and indicating adjoining parcels and possible easements and right of way.

The Articles of Incorporation

Most states consider a condominium association to be unincorporated and thus do not require the developer to record its articles of incorporation. In states where they must be filed, the articles set up the condominium association as a corporation (usually a nonprofit one) under the laws of the state.

When an association is incorporated, the individual members cannot be personally liable for any actions taken by the association. The articles also provide guidelines for the association's administrative functions. In addition to filing articles of incorporation for the single condominium association, the developer also may file articles of incorporation to form a master association.

A master association, also called a common association, is a nonprofit corporation that owns and is responsible for recreational facilities shared by residents of several condominium developments. For example, a single condominium community may not be large enough to support recreational amenities, while on the other hand three communities very close in proximity may be. The developer, therefore, may set aside a separate section of land conveniently located to these communities to build a swimming pool and tennis courts. He or she then would file articles of incorporation to establish a master association that would be responsible for the facilities' maintenance, repair, and operation. The articles of incorporation of a master association should state that each of the participating condominiums' unit owners automatically is a member, each has a vote in the decision-making process, and each is responsible for a share of the expenses.

The Bylaws

The declaration and the articles of incorporation create the condominium association and give it its legal power. The bylaws, sometimes known as the code of regulations, state how this authority may be exercised. The declaration establishes a broad administrative framework for the association, while the bylaws provide rules for handling routine matters. The two documents may cover similar subjects and at first glance appear to duplicate each other; however, the bylaws usually are more detailed, outlining specific procedures for the administration of the association and the day-to-day operation of the condominium community. Again, because state requirements vary, the content of the bylaws may vary from state to state.

The bylaws should be drafted to accommodate future needs and potential problems. Procedures for making changes in the bylaws may be written into either the declaration or the bylaws themselves. Although the bylaws generally are easier to amend than the declaration, this document also should be prepared carefully by the developer and his attorney in order to set up an administratively sound association.

The Unit Deed

The individual unit deed is the document that legally transfers the title of a condominium unit and its undivided portion of the common areas from the developer to the purchaser. Similar to the contract signed by the buyer of a traditional single-family house, it outlines the basic provisions of a contract of sale. These include the purchase price, a description of the unit that is being purchased and of any easements, the conditions of the sale, the percentage of the common areas that is being purchased, and any other specifications required by state law or the particular condominium project.

There is, however, one key clause that distinguishes the unit deed from the deed to a conventional house. It states that *the purchaser has received copies of the declaration, bylaws, house rules and regulations, and any other pertinent documents. In effect, the unit deed includes samples of the documents related to it. When the new unit owner signs the agreement, he acknowledges that he has read the documents and accepts all of there provisions.*

In addition to the principal governing documents, the file that is submitted with the unit deed might include an initial operating budget, a management agreement, recreational leases, and maintenance or service contracts. These are disclosed in an effort to alert consumers to possible abuse by the developer and enable them to make decisions about the purchase accordingly.

An initial operating budget should indicate clearly the cost of operating the association, maintaining the common areas, providing common services as well as reserves. The initial budget often is used as a sales tool to indicate to the buyer the cost and complexities of operating common areas. If the developer underestimates the budget either accidentally or intentionally, or subsidizes the project, the buyer may believe maintenance costs to be much lower than they actually are. Therefore, the developer should prepare his budget carefully and honestly with professional assistance to avoid the association's being faced with drastic increases after it assumes control of the common areas. Great care must be taken so that the association members have a minimum operating deficit at the time the developer has completed the project.

A condominium management agreement is a contract between a professional management firm or developer representative of the condominium project. It outlines those management functions for which the firm is responsible and indicates the rates of compensation. This disclosure gives prospective buyers the opportunity to identify any contracts calling for excessive lengths of service or excessive rates of compensation. Any service contracts with outside contractors to perform maintenance tasks or deliver common services should be disclosed.

Rules and Regulations

The rules and regulations are the guidelines to day-today personal behavior, and each resident of the condominium community is required to comply with their restrictions. They tell the residents how they must conduct themselves in the common areas and also may include measures that affect relations among neighbors.

The rules and regulations are based on the provisions of the governing documents. The developer initially submits them to purchasers with the other documents. However, as association members gain experience in living in the condominium community, they may wish to change, or add regulations.

What is contained in the Governing Documents:

While laws governing condominium ownership vary from state to state, governing documents everywhere commonly deal with certain general subjects:

(1) the definition of the individual units and the common areas.
(2) the method of determining percentages of ownership interest in the common areas.
(3) the creation of the association and an outline of its administrative procedures.
(4) maintenance responsibilities.
(5) management requirements.
(6) the assessment system and other fiscal policies.
(7) insurance requirements and damage or destruction provisions.
(8) rules, regulations, and restrictions.
(9) the transfer of control from the developer to the association. A checklist that notes which subjects are treated in which documents can be a valuable reference.

The declaration defines the common areas, the buildings, grounds, and other facilities in which every unit owner has an undivided interest and it identifies the individual units. The condominium units occasionally are defined merely as all the property that is not owned in common with all the other condominium unit owners. Usually, however, the unit is defined in very specific terms. The following is an example of the detail that can be used in defining a condominium unit:

Unit shall mean an individual air space unit which is contained within the unfinished perimeter walls, floors, ceilings, windows, and doors, together with all interior non supporting walls, fixtures, and improvements therein contained, and those installations within such air space unit for electricity, gas, water, and heating, including, but not limited to, pipes, wires, ducts, cables, conduits, public utility lines, equipment, tanks, boilers, and hot water heaters, pumps, motors, fans, and compressors *which serve only the individual unit* and do not serve any other unit, commencing at the point at which such installations enter the unit; provided that the unit shall not include any of the foundations, roof, columns, girders, beams, or other structural components of the building as shown on the condominium map or any other common areas as hereinafter defined. Similarly, although common areas are occasionally defined as all property other than the individual units, they usually are defined in much greater detail. Typically, they include the land upon which the condominium project is constructed; the foundations, load-bearing walls, columns, girders, beams, supports, and roofs; exterior surfaces; steps, lobbies, halls, stairways, entrances, fire escapes, exits, and communication ways; yards, private streets, parking areas, garages, and open-space gardens; the clubhouse, pool, and other recreational facilities; central utility services that are part of the common areas or that serve more than one unit; elevators, garbage containers, and incinerators; and any enclosed air spaces in the building that are not included within a unit.

Any limited common areas that may exist also are described in the declaration. Limited common areas are those that are physically part of the common areas but reserved for the exclusive use of a specific unit owner or group of owners. Legal definitions of limited common areas vary among states. In some, areas defined as limited common areas might include a patio or balcony attached to a unit, a storage locker, a parking space, an outside front door, or stairs leading to a single unit. However, at least one state's laws classify these elements as the property of the individual unit owner, even though they are not within the boundaries of the unit. Some states recognize as limited common areas such elements as corridors or stairways that lead to a group of units and are designed for the exclusive use of the residents of those units. Whatever the requirements of a given state, the declaration of a condominium should define the limited common areas accordingly.

Units and common areas also should he described in the individual unit deeds. However, the unit deed definitions may be less detailed than the declaration definitions or may even simply refer to the declaration to identify the unit. The unit deed also usually defines a unit by reference to its post office address and the corresponding unit number on the condominium plat.

Determine Ownership Interest

The method for assigning percentages of ownership interest may be determined solely by the developer. However, most states have developed guidelines that he or she must follow. A unit owner's percentage of ownership interest usually is based either on the area that the unit covers, on its original value or just divided by the number of units in a community.. The later method is considered to be the more equitable way of assessing financial responsibilities. Because value is relative, the value method seldom is used anymore to determine ownership interest. Both the declaration and the unit deed should clearly indicate that the percentage of interest in the common areas is undivided and that the owner cannot sever his share of the common areas. The unit and its accompanying percentage of ownership also are inseparable and must be conveyed together whenever the unit is resold.

Although the percentages of ownership interest usually remains constant once they are determined, a declaration may contain a provision that would allow the percentages to be changed. Changes in ownership interest usually occur in conjunction with expandable condominium projects.

An expandable condominium project is one that is designed to permit the developer to add additional multifamily living structures to the original structure or structures. For example, a developer may wish to give himself a chance to assess demand for condominium units before committing her or himself to building the maximum number of units a project can consist of. To permit himself this option, the developer may include a clause in the declaration that would permit changes in the percentages of ownership interest in the event of expansion of the project.

Establish Administrative Procedures

No community can run efficiently and successfully without some sort of orderly government. The condominium community is no exception. A condominium association is created to fill the need for government. The bylaws of the association usually establish most administrative procedures. Because most states require the bylaws to be submitted with the declaration, the declaration usually will discuss association issues in general terms only, referring the unit owner to the bylaws for specific rules of operation. Articles of incorporation also may provide certain administrative guidelines.

The declaration usually does two things to establish administrative procedures. It usually recognizes the board of directors, sometimes referred to as a board of trustees, indicates how many votes each unit owner is entitled to. For example, each owner may be entitled to a number of votes equal to his percentage of ownership interest. Alternately, a one-unit, one-vote rule may be applied.

The various governing documents may outline additional administrative procedures, such as the method of election of the board of directors, the number of board members and their qualifications, their terms of office, and the powers and duties of the hoard. They should specify which officers are to be elected (usually, a president, vice president, secretary, and treasurer), their duties, and the method of election. The documents also should establish the association rules for calling meetings, requirements for notifying members of meetings, voting procedures, and a model order of business for the annual membership meeting. They also may contain provisions relating to such matters as filling vacancies on the board, removing directors, calling and conducting hoard meetings, and establishing a committee system.

Because of the differences among state laws, some of these provisions may be found in the bylaws in one state and in the declaration in another state. Careful review of all the governing documents is essential to fully understand how the association will operate.

Outline Maintenance Responsibilities

The governing documents should specify which maintenance responsibilities belong to the individual unit owner and which belong to the association to assure that clear lines are drawn between common and individual expenses. They should state clearly that the unit owner is liable for the costs of all maintenance and repairs inside his unit, including the costs of redecorating, upkeep of interior surfaces of windows and doors, most utilities (in some condominiums, certain utilities are provided by the association), and any other costs that affect his unit. They should further state that the condominium association is obligated to operate and maintaining the common areas, perhaps listing the services for which the association is directly responsible. These services might include, among others, the provision of water, sewer services, trash collection, and all utility services to the common areas, as well as the provision of materials and labor necessary to operation of the common areas. **A tip about trash removal:** You probably are paying taxes right now on trash removal and still paying one of the largest expenditures for your community, private trash pick up. Many communities have been successful in getting the city or township to pick up there trash. Now, there may be some things that need to be altered to conform with the local pick up, like specified pick up locations, fencing around those area etc. but you would save considerably if the city picked up your trash. Do yourself a favor and look at the amount of money projected for the trash pick up and have the manager ask about this on the local level.

Delegate Management Authority

Although the board of directors is ultimately responsible for managing the condominium, most condominium documents, usually in either the declaration or the bylaws, specify that the association may hire a professional management agent to assist the board in fulfilling its duties. Some documents may authorize the board to delegate any or all of its duties to an agent; others may list the duties that the board may delegate. Some may include further provisions for canceling an agent's contract, requiring unit owner approval of an agent's contract, or limiting the length of an agent's contract.

Establish Fiscal Procedures

Running a condominium association can be a very expensive undertaking. Fortunately, the legal documents provide a means for adequately funding the operation by outlining procedures for assessing unit owners for common expenses. The documents require the association to adopt a yearly budget based upon the estimated cost of maintaining and repairing the common areas and operating the association. Each unit owner is assessed his or her share of this cost based upon their percentage of ownership interest. The documents should state how the assessments should be collected and may offer guidelines for penalizing delinquent unit owners and setting limits on assessment levels without a owners majority consent. This could be a problem as discussed previously in the amendment portion. The documents also may specify how often assessments are to be collected.

An important fiscal responsibility of the association is to establish reserve funds. Most documents require it to set up two reserve funds: a capital reserve fund for the repair and replacement of common areas and facilities and an operating contingency reserve fund to cover emergencies and unusual expenditures that are not anticipated when the annual budget is drafted. Because these reserves may not be sufficient to cover all emergencies, the documents usually include provisions for making special assessments(group loud scream.)

The governing documents often contain guidelines for internal fiscal controls. For example, they may require that financial records be audited each year, that all checks be signed by two people, specifically designated by the board of directors, and that with reasonable notice, those financial records be made available to any unit owner who wants to review them.

Outline Insurance Requirements

Individual unit owners are responsible for their privately owned unit. However, responsibility for protecting common areas from liability falls to the association through its board of directors. Determining how to adequately insure all the elements that make up a condominium raises certain questions. Although the documents cannot provide all the answers, they should offer guidelines to help the association protect itself against liability.

Declarations usually outline a set of basic insurance requirements, varying widely in the degree to which they are detailed. Some offer broad generalizations, others precise specifications. In general, most documents require an association to obtain adequate physical damage insurance coverage against fire and certain other calamities, to carry liability insurance. Some outline guidelines for obtaining appropriate amounts of physical damage and liability coverage.

The declaration should outline steps for repairing or replacing common areas in the event of fire or other casualty. It also may prescribe how to obtain bids for the repair or reconstruction of damaged common areas, how to levy special assessments against unit owners if insurance proceeds are insufficient, and how to handle reconstruction funds, the unit owners may not wish to rebuild a project that is destroyed or badly damaged; the declaration should establish ground rules for dealing with such a situation. Declarations commonly hold that if a large portion of the project is destroyed, the condominium association does not have to rebuild it, providing that a certain percentage of unit owners agree that it need not. This clause also may specify how insurance proceeds and any other funds held by the association are to be distributed if the association were terminated.

Establish Rules, Regulations, and Restrictions

The success of the condominium community depends in large part on the rules, regulations, and restrictions that govern how residents are expected to conduct themselves. Typically, the declaration subjects all unit owners to general covenants, while the bylaws and house rules and regulations provide specific guides to day-to-day living. Without these restrictions and a means to enforce them, condominium living would become chaotic. The condominium community must have two categories of restrictions: use restrictions and architectural restrictions. The former attempt to regulate human behavior; the latter outline procedures a unit owner must follow if he or she wishes to change the outward appearance of their unit. Both sets of restrictions are essential to the proper use of common areas and the preservation of the design and character of the condominium development. In addition to specifying rules, regulations, and restrictions, the documents also may specify how violations should be treated.

Use restrictions may appear in the declaration, bylaws, and/or rules and regulations. Use restrictions usually indicates those rules that are prohibitive. For example, use restrictions may prohibit loud noises, certain kinds or sizes of pets, obstruction of the common areas, trash accumulation in the common areas, or construction of outdoor structures on the common areas.

Restrictions are essential to the protection of the community's character and rightly belong in one of the principle documents. Rules and regulations that relate to day-to-day living, on the other hand, may be subject to more frequent change. Therefore, the board of directors typically is authorized to modify, delete, or adopt new rules and regulations. Subjects covered by rules and regulations usually include such matters as parking, the conduct of children and pets, noise levels, guest provisions, and use of common areas for personal use. House rules and regulations may include or be supplemented by rules and regulations governing any recreational facilities. For example, a set of swimming pool rules might restrict breakable glass from the pool area, or require children under a certain age to be accompanied by an adult. Other sets of rules might regulate use of a clubhouse or tennis court.

Architectural restrictions or controls are designed to protect the condominium's character and, hopefully, to enhance its value. The standards they set for design, material, color, and use are not intended to stifle individual freedom or creativity but to preserve the project's original design. To adequately fulfill the purpose of protecting the condominium's value, architectural restrictions should be extremely detailed. Here, for example, is a detailed set of restrictions drawn from one set of bylaws:

It shall be prohibited to install, erect, attach, apply, paste, hinge, screw, nail, build, alter, remove, or construct any lighting, shades, screens, awnings. patio covers, decorations, fences, aerials, antennas, radio or television broadcasting or receiving devices, slabs, sidewalks, curbs, gutters, patios, porches, driveways, walls, or to make any change or otherwise alter, including alteration in color, in any manner whatsoever to the exterior of any condominium unit or upon any of the common elements within the project until the complete plans and specifications showing the color, height, material, type of construction, another proposal for change shall have been submitted to and approved in writing as to the harmony of external design, color, and location in relation to surrounding structures and topography by the board of directors or by an architectural community designated by it.

Almost without exception, condominium documents require the board of directors to form an architectural control committee. This committee generally is responsible for reviewing and recommending to the board of directors approval or rejection of applications for exterior architectural changes or making the decisions itself.

The Board Meeting

Let's talk about board meetings. Properly conducted meetings provide reasonably discussed differences of opinion while dealing with and proceeding with administrative needs. The ultimate effectiveness of board meetings or annual meeting of the membership for election depends on the creation of and adherence to fair sensible pertinent guidelines. To assure that all meetings run smoothly the agenda should be planned and followed. One of the keys to board members effectiveness is PREPARATION. To be sure you are prepared, the agenda and meeting packet (including all information to be discussed per the agenda) should be distributed to all board members in a reasonable time prior to a meeting. BE PREPARED. If you think you need more information from the managing agent or a resident based on the information provided in the packet, call the manager to see if that can be provided to the members prior to the meeting. Do most of you on a board or committee get your packet of information prior to the meeting? A WELL ORGANIZED AGENDA FACILITATES THE DEMOCRATIC PROCESS AND STIMULATES IDEAS AND OPINIONS.

Now, about notifications of meetings so that unit owners may attend, we all know the importance of attendance for elections are but boards are almost always reluctant to solicit member attendance at the regular board meetings. I understand how and why that occurs but the truth is the membership must be notified of the meetings. HOLDING OPEN MEETINGS ASSURES THE INTEGRITY OF THE BOARD..(female scream)I know…I know…I understand how you feel about it, but it is the forum where owners can speak to and hear the board directly. Again BE PREPARED, if an owner wishes to address the board at the meeting on a specific topic or situation, they should make that request in writing and state the nature of the discussion. It can then be appropriately researched and placed on the agenda and the board as well as the managing agent can be prepared with any necessary information pertaining to that matter.

To encourage homeowner participation regular board meeting should be held at the same time and day each month, i.e. first Monday of the month at 7:30. Most board meetings are held in the evening so as to not only accommodate the working board members but the residents as well.

Following parliamentary procedure is essential to a successful meeting. I urge you to follow "Roberts' Rules of Order," that book is available in all bookstores. These procedures are *essential* for the control necessary to transact business and protect owner's rights. It does seem to make meetings much more complicated at times but ..it is designed to be sure everyone agrees or discussion is made on the item and then the minutes reflect a board that has entertained all the discussions before making a judgement.

One of the ways to help the board facilitate the business of the association is to assign committees. Committees should be assigned for specific tasks. They do the research and then report to the board on their findings and make recommendations to the BOD. REMEMBER, NO BOARD CAN FUNCTION ADAQUATLY WITHOUT THE ASSISTANCE OF OTHERS. I'm not talking about assistance by the managing agent or other professionals in specific fields but the association membership is composed of members with a wide range of talents. Bankers, insurance professionals, construction workers, painters and business owners with a variety of expertise. Try to tap into that talent and get them involved. Granted getting them to volunteer may be almost impossible but committees are and have always been an excellent source of guidance for a BOD and a way to train future association leaders. Committees are created to recommend changes in the implementation of policies, they do not establish policy. That is the responsibility of the BOD. You are looking for their help and time to gather information and make a reasonable recommendation based on that research and their knowledge. There are many areas where committees should be established: Architectural control, landscaping, grounds, budget/finance, insurance, maintenance, rules and regulations, newsletter/communications, recreational facilities, lakes, and even a transition committee if the developer has not fully turned all property and control over to the community. I do recommend that one member of the BOD serve on each committee if at all possible. If not, certainly the chair of that committee should know the proper procedures to follow and should attend the regular board meetings to make the committee report. Now something very important.. all board members should have past history of issues, so make sure you have copies of minutes of previous meetings and pertinent information that was included with the minutes. A list of all current committees including members names and meeting schedule, in case you wanted to attend and observe. The board should also request a copy of their agenda and minutes of their meetings. You should have any rule handbook including architectural guidelines used and distributed to the unit owners.

One more thing is essential as a board member, A SENSE OF HUMOR! If you can't laugh at some of the situations before you, you won't last as a board member. The stress must be relieved somehow. The ability to laugh at the countless hours devoted to residents about dog poop, unit owner disputes with each other, kids riding bikes on the tennis courts, cats digging up neighbors flower gardens and how many inches the landscapers cut the grass, is really essential. That is not to say some of these things are not valid but you need to step back sometimes and look at the whole picture and just see the humor in it.

Planning for the meeting

Successful meetings don't just happen they are carefully planned!

Once the legal criteria has been met and the homeowners have "taken over" the association development, the manager will work with a board comprised of only homeowners. To insure the effectiveness of board meetings, it is essential that the manager educate board members to recognize that the association is a business which must make sound business decisions, a mini-government which must provide services and enact rules, and a judicial body which must enforce covenants or levy fines for the violation of covenants is the responsibility of the board of directors.

The law prescribes that it is the board which is ultimately responsible for the administration of the community association by the meeting process. The board may employ a manager as its agent to carry out certain prescribed duties, but as in all agency relationships, the board is ultimately accountable. The board can sue and be sued. The board and the manager must ensure that board meetings are planned and executed in a highly professional manner.

The first step in planning a meeting is to select the place, date and time of the meeting, preferably in that order. Since the manager cannot schedule all meetings to meet the convenience of all homeowners, the best approach is to research these following matters carefully:

Place for the Meeting

Ideally, meetings of' community association should be conducted within the community. A clubhouse on the property is ideal. Neutral locations and preferable to a board member's home. If' it is necessary to go outside the community, meeting rooms often are available at local schools. Pick a location which is comfortable, appropriate in size, handicapped accessible and one which should produce a minimum number of interruptions during the meeting. A private room at the clubhouse presumably would be preferable to a private home where children, telephones and pets may produce frequent interruptions. Of course it's not true that a filled room indicates a successful event! —but, if a room seats 200 persons and 15 are present there is a sense of failure. On the other hand, if' a room seats 20 persons and 15 are present, an initial positive impression has been made. Fill the same room with 25 persons and you have a "great impression!" When selecting a meeting location the manager should take into consideration the anticipated attendance and choose a room which conforms as closely as possible to that number. Review the lighting capabilities of the location. Will the room be comfortably heated or cooled? Are the seats reasonably comfortable? Be sure to check whether other activities will be scheduled in rooms adjacent to the one where the board meeting will take place.

Date For the Meeting.

Most community association meetings should be conducted on weekdays. Avoid Friday, Saturday or Sunday meeting dates. In selecting a date be sure to check the calendar so as to avoid legal holidays, religious events or events of great appeal such as the Oscars.

Time for the Meeting.

The best time for a meeting which traditionally is the time which produces the largest community association attendance—is 7:30 p.m. This hour allows the homeowner the opportunity to get home from work and to eat dinner—but it does not give the homeowner the chance to get too comfortable with television or a good book. The only exceptions to this might be communities where the majority of owners are retired.

Encouraging Meeting Attendance.

Having selected the place, date and time for the meeting, announce it publicly and scheduled in advance so people can plan accordingly so other committees do not schedule events which conflict with the board meetings. Choose, for example, the third Thursday of each month and identify this date to all members of the homeowner community. This later date in the month may be more advantageous because you will also have a more current delinquency report. Mark it clearly in the community newsletters, on posters and on the manager's office calendar. The internet is also a great way to post meetings. Let the new technology work for you by creating a web page for your community. You can use a free home page maker like AOL Press or personal publisher etc. and get the word out this way. The most important factor is the encouragement of homeowner participation and attendance. The manager and the president of the BOD are typically responsible for getting board members to meetings. A good reminder can be sent a week in advance of the meeting date.

The Proposed Agenda and The Final Agenda:

Asking for input on the agenda. The president, the treasurer and certainly the manager have progress reports which should be included with the agenda. A few days before the meeting the agenda, along with any pertinent information for the meeting, should be sent to all board members. The manager should help the board members realize that their input and active participation is expected before, during and after all board meetings. Every good meeting has a written agenda. It is a program, it must be organized and it must reflect planning. It can instill confidence. It shows the homeowner that there are goals to be met. Have sufficient copies of the agenda available for all board members, plus additional copies for the anticipated number of homeowners who may come to observe the meeting. Of course, the agenda must be followed and the manager, especially in the association's formative months, should have a working knowledge of parliamentary procedure so that the items on the agenda can be expedited. When necessary, the agenda should also provide for input from the association's lawyer, insurance agent, auditor or other needed professional. Every agenda should provide time for the manager's report. This is an important communications link with the community. It should include a review of assignments completed and pending. To do otherwise is to invite misunderstanding or distrust. Most board meetings take place monthly and this affords the manager an excellent opportunity to give a timely accounting of his or her accomplishments for the community.

Remember: *The agenda distributed to unit owners attending the meeting may contain persons' names and addresses on most issues, but should never contain the names and/or addresses of delinquent accounts. Only the BOD and the manager can be privy to that information, not even in the newsletter.*

Inform committee chairpersons that, while their written reports will be requested on the agenda, the BOD expect their appearance at board meetings. Develop the attitude that written reports are not substitutes for personal attendance. If a committee chairperson cannot attend the board meeting, then another member of that committee should be in attendance to present the report on the chairperson's behalf. Chronic absenteeism at meetings does not benefit the community. The board may choose to initiate a rule with a set number consecutive meetings missed and calling for resignation. Usually this is three(3) consecutive missed meetings and that carries over to committee members as well. Of course it is always up the board to evaluate each situation, i.e. if the absenteeism's was due to an illness or surgery etc.

Encouraging Community Attendance

The community association board makes its decisions through the reports and recommendations of the manager as well as standing and ad hoc committees. In addition, personal homeowner attendance should be strongly encouraged. The manager can do this by announcing the meeting, not once or twice, but several times through several different methods.

The manager must educate the board members to understand that the board meeting is not a war zone. Homeowners must be encouraged to attend and observe the board at work. Many communities have found a workable format for conducting board meetings without homeowner interruptions by allocating a set time at the start of a meeting or more customary at the end of the meeting for homeowner input. With good board leadership this can prove to be a most effective arrangement.

Another means of encouraging homeowner attendance is for the president to permit limited input from homeowner attendees as board discussion takes place. This procedure is workable only if the president is a strong leader who has no hesitation in cutting off homeowners who interrupt or comments which may go on and on and become aimless. The combination of both methods, that is, homeowner input at appropriate times, plus input at, preferably, the conclusion of the meeting, often results in a very productive meeting. It tends to reduce complaints and increases homeowner satisfaction because homeowners feel they have a viable forum in which to be heard.

All presidents of the board will not be good presiding officers. Because of this it is important that the manager have a knowledge of meeting mechanics so that the president can be guided by the manager into more efficient presiding techniques. *Every association should own these two books, "Roberts' rules of order" and "Become an effective Condo Board Member."* A brief review of the "game plan" by the manager and president prior to the meeting may help the presiding officer. Also, it is important that managers sit next to the president during meetings and guide him or her through the agenda. While these techniques will not insure the president's improvement as a presiding officer, they should help to keep the meetings on schedule and moving in a positive direction. The question then arises: what is the manager's role in meetings? Is he or she to actively participant or sit and quietly watch? The answer to the question depends on the competence of the manager and the degree of knowledge and experience achieved by the board president. The manager, if working with fairly new board members, should take an active role in recommending agendas which reflect proper topics for discussion, and should help keep meetings on a positive theme. It is for this reason that board Members terms are staggered. So that not all members come up for re-election at the same time. When the board uses its meetings to effectively administer a business, mini-government and judicial body, the manager should be able to simply present management reports and have little involvement in the conduct of the meeting.

The Meeting Process

Follow "Roberts' rules of order."

The Call to Order and the Adjournment.

The presiding officer of the Association calls the meeting to order and calls for the motion to adjourn the meeting. Nothing can discourage board participation and homeowner attendance as effectively as meetings which begin late and/or meetings which never end! In courtesy to those present, a meeting called for 7:30 p.m. should begin at 7:30 p.m. Begin the meeting late this month, and everyone can conclude that the meetings will begin late next month. There can be no exceptions: meetings must begin on time!

Similarly, meetings must not drag on into the late hours of the evening. No association is so busy that its meetings cannot be concluded in two and one-half to three hours. Thus, a meeting called for 7:30 p.m. should end no later than 9:30 p.m. with an additional one-half or one hour for community input. Set a 9:30 p.m. limit and, surprisingly, that goal will be met.

Once finalized, the minutes of the association board must be preserved. This is a legal requirement. In addition, members of the association should have these minutes available for review whenever they desire to read them. Perhaps the most appropriate location for the preservation of minutes is the manager's office, since officers of the association change from time to time while the office of manager continues from year to year. The board secretary should also retain copies of the minutes.

The board minutes contain objectives to be achieved by the association. These objectives range from the solving of individual homeowner maintenance problems to policy decisions regarding the investment of reserve funds. Because of this, it is important that the manager and officers of the association establish a follow-up procedure to insure that board meeting directives are carried out. Check lists of projects to be completed by the various groups which should be maintained with corresponding time tables for the projects. Presumably the manager will be in charge of those items which are normally his or her responsibility. It should be noted that while the board can delegate responsibility for various projects, it cannot delegate his accountability for the proper completion of the projects.

Communications During Board Meetings

During the flow of the meeting process, the manager and the chairman will have many opportunities to exercise leadership. These are some of the specific points that can be helpful during the meeting.

a) Help keep discussions on the target. Valuable time is lost when discussions stray from the main purpose. "Getting back to the motion, I would like to make a couple of observations."

b) Offer alternatives when discussions stall. Be prepared when the members seem to be hesitant to discuss business. This can happen for many reasons and the proper verbal response will depend on the situation. It might be helpful to appoint a committee with a board member as chairperson to research this topic and present a recommendation to the next meeting of the board. There seems to be some hesitancy to carry these discussions further, "would it help to have more information?" "There seems to be three parts to this issue which are not clear. Perhaps if each one is discussed they will fall in place."

c) Check prior board actions. Boards change year to year. Some of the same topics will be raised each year by new members of the board. Be alert to these topics and call to the attention of the board the dates and minutes where these items were discussed and what actions were taken. Do this in a non-threatening manner to be informative rather than judgmental. It is difficult to experience this year after year without losing patience.

d) Watch the clock. When it is necessary, you might say, " I see that we have several agenda items left to cover and we have ten minutes to the agreed adjournment time?" Encourage time schedules and to refer to them throughout the meeting.

e) Be alert to proposed actions that might be in conflict with the bylaws of the association. This occasion arises when discussing policy. Select your words carefully and be factual. Keep a set of the bylaws at hand. To see a possible conflict between this proposed policy and the bylaws of the association suggest that "prior to adoption, the association attorney be consulted." Read the item from the bylaws to support your point.

f) Urge consistency in actions of the board. Maintain your records so that you might be able to refer back to them in urging the board to be consistent.

g) Be fair. Under pressure from one or more association member pressing for a particular point of view, the board may act inappropriately. As an example, a friend of a board member demands that teens be restricted in the use of the swimming pool during the hours that he or she normally swims. Complaining about the noise and water fights in the pool. You need to stall a rash decision and be sure you have all the facts: "Has anyone talked with the young people who have been involved?" " Is this something that happens regularly or an occasional incident?" Perhaps before making a decision in this matter the board might ask the manager to investigate the matter further and report back to the board.

h) Management reports are more effective if key points in the report are verbalized and the report in its entirety is presented to each member of the board several days prior to the meeting. Short, informational statements enable the listener to gain an overall view of the total report and pinpoint areas for questions. Responding to questions and requests for further explanation avoids lengthy statements and over justification for actions.

Communications During Homeowner Business Meetings:

1. Prepare key persons and leaders prior to the meeting. Clarify in your own mind a purpose for the meeting.
2. Be sure that person understands the purpose of the meeting and is able to verbalize it. This can be achieved simply by asking the chairman for what he or she considered the purpose of the meeting. If he has difficulty stating it, you might help him. Point out the legal aspects of the meeting and have appropriate back-up materials for reference. It is important that the chairperson will be able to state his or her goals as well as the purpose of the meeting. The goal should be a specific statement, usually action-oriented. Communicate with homeowners as to their expectations for the meeting and verbalize these to the presiding person.
3. If homeowner input to the meeting is desired, the manager can help the chairperson set the format for the meeting to allow for as much member involvement as possible. "We are interested in what each of you has to say about the topic of the evening. Please keep your remarks directly to the topic and keep them as brief as you can." "The chair reserves the right to limit any speaker who prolongs a statement." "The chair requests that individuals refrain from responding to any one statement made until all persons present had

the opportunity to speak." Express appreciation for the time and the effort given by those present. End the meeting on a positive note.

4. The results of meetings must be communicated to the homeowners. As previously stated, meetings do not take place in a vacuum. After they are planned and executed, it is imperative that the results of the meeting, especially a board meeting, be communicated to all homeowners, both those residing within the community and those absentee owners. Share the success of the evening with others who are not present through the newsletter, internet, bulletin board etc. The non-resident homeowner pays a monthly assessment and is responsible for their unit and has a right to expect that all communications distributed to resident homeowners also will be distributed to him or her.

5. Copies of the board minutes should be distributed to all board members and committee chairpersons, to the association's lawyer, to the manager and to other designated persons. A full text of all board meeting minutes should be preserved permanently. The minutes along with other pertinent information should be filed on site preferably in the manager's office where any homeowner may read them at any time, given reasonable notice and minutes can also be posted on bulletin boards. Don't forget the internet as well. On your communities home page.

Perhaps the most reliable and inexpensive way of informing homeowners about board meeting results is through the association newsletter. Here the minutes can be summarized, important figures can be disclosed, and major actions can be explained.

Architectural Controls

Every homeowner has a right to the exclusive enjoyment of his or her unit but does not have the right to make changes to the exterior of that unit which would affect the appearance of the community. Architectural controls are imposed on each member and that is usually the cause of many problems within a community. Most governing documents require an architectural committee to review any proposed changes to the exterior and offer guidelines-(final approval made by the BOD.)

The first step in the approval process is to require each unit owner who wishes to modify the exterior of their unit, to provide a completed architectural application along with any other relevant forms so that the committee can properly review and make a ruling.

In order to speed reviews and assure consistent decisions the committee must adopt community standards. Relating to such things as, patios, gardens, plantings, laundry hanging on balconies, screen doors-in other words anything that can be done by an owner and can be seen outside by another unit owner. Once standards are adopted the review should be systematic. *Standards ensure that all unit owners will be treated equally.* Owners participation should be encouraged when standards are being developed and reviewed, this will encourage there acceptance. Problems in enforcement always arise. Although applications are required for modifications some unit owners bypass this requirement. It is important to follow up and issue strong warnings and any other legal remedies until the unit owner has complied.

The job of adopting guidelines does not finish the job of the BOD, now you must properly get the word out to all unit owners. *Rules that have not been properly announced are no rules at all.* The board cannot expect compliance. Get out that notice, mail it to all owners, get it in the newsletter, post it in the office or bulletin board, create an internet web page for your community and post any new rule. Do whatever you can do to notify the homeowners, absentee or resident, of that new guideline.

Develop a handbook of rules and regulations and distribute it to each homeowner. As additional rules are approved distribute them to all owners to include with their handbook, (be sure to number the amended or additional page and date it with the date it was approved by the BOD.) Make sure new homeowners receive an up to date handbook. Remember they should get the POS but your additions are not in that book so include all the additions in a handy handbook for new owners. Should push ever come to shove, you must show that the homeowner did receive notice of the guideline prior to his violation. Keep that in mind.

Happiness Condominium Association
Architectural Review Application

Date

Unit Owner

Address of Unit

Phone

Nature of Improvement

Color (if applicable)

Location (if applicable)

Dimensions (if applicable)

Planting Material (if applicable)—

(A sketch of all improvements must be attached to the application
To show location and dimensions.)

For Internal Use Only
Date Received
Reviewed on—
Status.......................
Reason if not approved

Effective Communications

Residents need to be approached for their opinions and ideas. Feedback is essential. Without it there is no two-way communications. Owners should be urged to attend the board meetings so that direct face-to-face comments can take place. Questionnaires and surveys are also useful tools. Owners must be encouraged to share their views on how to solve the association's problems. The use of questionnaires and surveys, provides a way for members to make their opinions known. Some residents are more comfortable with this method of expressing their feelings than they are with direct contact. As for volunteers, the most important volunteer group is the board of directors itself. The board establishes a open climate of responsiveness to the members' appeals for help.

If the board is realistic in its expectations and continues to solicit feedback from the residents, those who show interest can often be recruited to serve as volunteers. By ensuring that the volunteers receive credit for their contributions when they do become involved and are recognized in the community at large, then the board will promote continued active support. *Membership involvement is essential to balance the needs of the community with the governing power of the board.*

The most obvious methods to conduct a volunteer search are the newsletter, in-house mailings, notices on the bulletin board and again by using the internet.

The board must appeal to the basic motivations of the association membership.

The reasons for volunteering are as varied as the people who volunteer. Some who volunteer want to gain recognition, or accomplish something they feel is important. Others simply want to contribute to their community, while others seek to meet people and feel a part of a group activity. Some may simply be concerned with safety and security or their investment. In addition to initiating an individualized committee recruitment program the board should enlist the expertise of the manager.

Regardless of how a member's commitment is obtained, the secret to sustaining involvement lies in the awareness that *people volunteer because it satisfies a purpose or value to them.* Successful recruitment appeals to individual talents. The board should not become discouraged if initial response is mixed nor should they continue using a single recruitment method. If a response is weak it is time to try another method. The discovery of a successful combination often involves trying many methods.

An effective recruitment letter that refers to a particular, clearly defined project should express urgency and give deadlines. It should be specific in the need for the project completion if an active committee of concerned members is to be found. Care should be taken in wording the letter. An effective method of opening the recruitment letter is to catch the attention of the recipient by asking questions which directly relates to him or her, such as: How much to charge for the use of the clubhouse? Should we remodel the clubhouse? Should we have scrubs plantings around the tennis court? Should we have an aerator put in the lake?

Regardless of how well worded a notice may be, reinforcement and follow up are needed. After the letter has been sent to the membership the board members should personally try to recruit members who are known to have the ability sought or have expressed desire to serve.

Motivation for Volunteer Participation

The biggest challenge to the board is to motivate members to participate. Even the most preoccupied members can be induced to participate to some degree when involvement is presented in a way which links their personal interests to community concerns. This can often be done by educating the members of an impending crisis which will affect him or her unless they take action. For example, the members who regularly use the pool or other recreational facilities are the most likely to actively work to solve a problem which involves that amenity.

Absentee owner tenants may volunteer under some circumstances be persuaded to serve on a committee on a particular project provided the need of the association can be closely linked to their special concerns. A tenant may not be permitted to be a board member or even on certain other committees as indicated by your documents, but there may be a committee that they could help with. Programs for teenagers after school, clubhouse events, gardening committees. Each member's degree of desire for involvement and commitment to the community will depend his or her personal need for fulfillment, sense of responsibility to the community, and the degree of his or her involvement in other activities in personal or business life.

New homeowners often display high initial enthusiasm. Get them working on a committee. If properly approached, many can (and will) bring particular skills or talents to the association. Once involved, if a member experiences a satisfying return for his or her time and energy, they are likely to continue helping.

Committee Direction forms

Finance Budget Committee:

I. SCOPE:

    The Finance/Budget Committee is formed by the board of directors and reports directly to the board. They assist in all duties relative to the financial affairs and responsibilities of the board in the financial area.

II. GOAL:

    The goal of the Finance/Budget Committee is to assist the board in maintaining the associations financial affairs in a sound viable condition and to provide expertise and recommendations to the board to assure proper administration and use of association funds.

III. ORGANIZATION:

    Committee Chairperson is appointed by the board of directors to serve for a term of one year. Adequate number of committee members to effectively carry out assigned duties to be selected by the Committee Chairperson.

IV. RESPONSIBILITIES:

    A. Develop a budget preparation calendar and program with management for adoption by the BOD.

    B. Review potential CPA firms for audit and make recommendations to the BOD

    C. Review the annual audit and tax reports.

D.   Solicit committee budget requirements and incorporate into final budget a proposal with the management agent for presentation and adoption by the BOD. Assist the BOD by recommending procedures for processing and informing members of assessment increases.

E.   Monitor associations financial reports and report to the treasurer on any anticipated actual budget variances.

V.   Reports:

A written report of any recommended budget changes at least three days prior to the regularly scheduled BOD meeting.

Coordinate reports with the management agent's monthly financial statement which are to be provided three days prior to the BOD meeting.

VI.   Meetings:

Chairman or appointed representative to attend regularly scheduled BOD meetings, committee or subcommittee meetings, as required, to carry out the committee responsibility. A special budget meeting annually to be announced to the membership to allow for member participation on proposed budget. Meetings of the memberships as required, to assure proper communication and flow of information on financial matters.

Maintenance Committee

I. SCOPE:
    The Maintenance Committee is formed by the board of directors and reports directly to the BOD. The committee will provide expertise and guidance to the board in all areas of maintenance responsibilities, as defined, by the legal documents.

II. ORGANIZATION:
    Committee Chairman is appointed by the board of directors to serve for a term of one year. Adequate number of committee members a cover the committee responsibilities in the following categories:
    A. Grounds Maintenance
    B. Snow Removal
    C. Recreational Facilities
    D. Drives and Walkways
    E. Exterior of Buildings
    F. Interior of Buildings-Housekeeping
    G. Interior of Buildings-Physical plant
    H. Capitol Improvements

III. RESPONSIBILTY:
    A. Develop a maintenance program with the managing agent that meets the requirements and desires of the community.
    B. Work with the management agent in preparation of the final budget recommendations for the BOD.

C. Review specifications and bids for contracted work pre-formed, note problems, suggest actions and corrections to the management agent.

D. Inspect common area and elements regularly for work pre-formed, note problems, suggest action, and corrections to the management agent.

E. Recommend additions and/or improvements to the common area and elements to the BOD.

F. Provide recommendations to the BOD on policy and procedures for handling homeowner complaints and maintenance requests.

IV.　Goal:

The primary responsibility of the maintenance committee is to advise and assist the board in preserving and enhancing the physical environment of the development.

V.　REPORTS:

A written report to be provided to the BOD at least three days prior to the regularly scheduled Board meeting.

A written report to the managing agent on committee concerns on a regularly scheduled basis.

VI.　MEETINGS:

Chairperson or appointed representative to attend regularly scheduled board of director meetings. Committee or sub-committee meetings, as required, to carry out the committee responsibilities. The Committee as a whole shall meet once a month on a regularly scheduled basis as announced, to the membership.

Rules & Regulations/Guidelines Committee

I. SCOPE:
    The committee is appointed by the board of directors and reports directly to the board. The committee is to provide assistance in establishing and enforcing the associations rules and regulations as adopted by the board of directors.

II. GOAL:
    The goal of the committee is to preserve a high quality of living and to provide for good communication and reasonable approach in setting forth rules and regulations for the benefit of the members as a whole.

III. ORGANIZATION:
    Committee chairperson is appointed by the BOD to serve a term of one year. Adequate number of committee members to cover the committee responsibilities.

IV. RESPONSIBILITY:
    A. Be knowledgeable of the established rules and regulations.
    B. Periodically review rules and regulations for adequacy and application.
    C. Recommend changes or additions to rules and regulations for adoption to the board of directors.
    D. Recommend procedures for enforcement of rules and regulations to the BOD.

     E. Coordinate with the other committees in disseminating and reviewing rules and regulations with the members.

     F. Monitor member compliance with the rules and regulations.

     G. Keep a record of committee meetings in the form of minutes.

VI. REPORTS:

A written report to the BOD on any recommendations and to keep them a breast of changes developments, and committee activity.

VII. MEETINGS:

Chairperson or appointee representative to attend regularly scheduled board meetings. Committee meetings as required to carry out the committee's responsibilities.

Communication/Newsletter Committee

I. SCOPE

The committee is appointed by the BOD and reports directly to the board, providing assistance in informing residents of pertinent association activities.

II. ORGANIZATION

Committee Chairperson to be appointed by the BOD and to serve for a term of one year. Adequate number of committee members to be selected by the chairperson to effectively carry out assigned responsibility.

III. GOAL

The goal of the committee is to keep homeowners informed about their association, activities, and events in the community as well as other items of interest which they feel appropriate and in the best interest of the association.

IV. RESPONSIBILTY:

A. Prepare and publish a monthly community newsletter.

   1. Prepare format for newsletter.

   2. Select name and article selection procedure to be presented to the BOD.

B. Publish notices as required by the BOD.

C. Prepare a newsletter/communication committee budget for the BOD.

D. Provide additional communication services such as birth announcements, birthdays, welcome to new members etc.

E. Reports to the BOD at regular meetings.

Revitalizing Your Community

Are your board meetings regularly cancelled due to a lack of quorum? Is there a high monthly delinquency rate? Has your association's property value dropped? Do the property grounds appear run down? Is your community's bulletin board and other notices regularly ignored? Does the community throw parties that few attend? Are there many violations of the rules and regulations? Are there old junked up cars throughout the community? These are a few of the more obvious signs of a community that is not well managed and certainly is apathetic. Bear in mind no one symptom taken by itself means the community is not managed well or is apathetic.

Consider this situation, the association was hit with a three hundred percent mid year increase in insurance premiums. The board dipped into the community's reserve funds to cover the additional costs without ever informing the membership. The board's decision was almost immediately followed by a major problem with the pool equipment which required the outlay of a substantial amount of money. In an effort to raise the money to pay for the repair, the board issued a special assessment, (I hope you never have to do that.)

What started as apathy rapidly turned into antagonism and the board of directors was blamed for everything that had ever gone wrong. In retaliation, the majority of board members threatened to quit.

Scenarios like the one described above can be prevented. Although a community communications may have deteriorated considerably, all does not have to be lost, provided the board takes action to revitalize its community as soon as the first signs of apathy become apparent. *The board must be willing to acknowledge that a vitalized membership is the essential.* An honest assessment of a community's strengths and weaknesses will help the board identify the actions it must take if the association is to recover. Let me suggest ways to vitalize association membership and provides some techniques to enlist and keep the active volunteers who are the key to any revitalization effort.

Successfully functioning community associations do not just happen.

A thriving community is developed through conscious effort. The greatest single barrier to active community development is apathy. Apathy promotes a breakdown of cooperation and interaction among the board of directors, manager, and community members. Both board of directors and residents share the responsibilities for revitalizing an apathetic community. However, *it is the board which holds the key to revitalization.* Goals, strategies, organization and follow-through must be developed by the board of directors and communicated to the membership for growth and involvement.

Revitalization is helped if there is an "issue" or focus of concern. This focus could be outside the community such as a nearby zoning case, or inside the community such as a budget crisis, major repair or just a "new image" including a new logo or entry sign, landscaping including benches and/or waste paper baskets along a path, additional children's play area with swings, slide etc.(but remember the maintenance follow up on all your improvements).

Communication is the vital link to community cooperation; however, the amount of communication must be balanced, as too much or too little can have a negative effect on members. It is important that residents have a means of making their opinions known to the board of directors, particularly prior to the board's making a major decision.

To restore a sense of community vitality, the board must constantly report on accomplishments and progress, asking for further volunteer help for identified areas of need. Before beginning a search for committee volunteers, the board of directors must first have a definite need for a committee and have a written statement of the duties, responsibilities and goals of the committee.

A carefully thought-out recruitment program would include understanding why people volunteer, so that a campaign can be designed to respond to individual motivations. Once volunteers are found and a committee is formed, the board of directors must have realistic expectations for results, act upon committee recommendations and give recognition to members for service. The hardest step in revitalizing a community association is the first one. A board of directors that realizes that it needs to do some thing to turn things around still has a difficult time breaking the previous patterns of behavior and communications. Listed below are several approaches that boards of directors in other community associations have used successfully to start the revitalization process. Perhaps one of them will help your board to initiate its effort.

1. *ASK FOR IMPUT.* Show that you want it by mailing a meeting notice to the membership indicating the topics of interest at that evenings meeting. We want your suggestions before going ahead with programs and a lot of good ideas can be presented about how we should operate in the future. *We're willing to listen and you may even want to work on the committee that is dealing with a topic of your interest, specialty or concern.*

2. *APPEAL TO INDIVIDUAL SELF INTEREST.* Ask for help. Asking for owners to write us a letter, come to the next board meeting, or join a committee to make sure that your interests are being adequately considered when we have to make decisions in the interest of all. At the very least indicate the topics of interest and desired committee help in the newsletter..

3. *BE HONEST.* Be honored that their vote for you was a matter of trust and you know that you have a tremendous responsibility. *You have elected us to care for thousands of dollars of property values and make decisions on legal, insurance, tax, accounting and engineering matters that are totally foreign to many of us. With no special skill that we bring to this office-only a desire to serve and to do our best. But we cannot do it alone. We need your help. We particularly need the help of those of you who have special skills that can be contributed to the association. If you have expertise in finance, construction, organizational skills, engineering, or writing and art, we need your help. A vital association is marked by members who show concern for the association and by a board that promotes member awareness and responds to member concerns.*

4. *Remember Competent Managers reflect the attitude of both members and board.* Since both board and management derive their authority from the association members, the members must ultimately bear the responsibility (as well as foot the bill) for adverse effects of apathy. Lack of interest on the part of property owners creates a climate which opens the door to neglect or pursuit of self-interest by those who have the proxy of the members. Concerned members are frequently challenged with the need to revitalize an apathetic association. While it is possible for one or more concerned and dedicated members to bring about change, members on the board are in the best position to promote the revitalization process.

The board of directors of a community association holds the key to the continued healthy functioning of the community. Elected, in trust, by the association to provide direction which will benefit the community, the board's authority touches all areas of community life-financial, maintenance, administration and regulations. Board decisions in large measure determine the quality of life within a community. An effective board develops association goals and strategies, organizes programs, and follows through to unify and promote a healthy community. The manager and employees will respond to an active board in executing their responsibilities.

A certain amount of apathy is inherent in community associations and must be expected. Not all members can or will be actively involved in the operation of their community. People move into a community association for various reasons. Many members enter a condominium community because they seek carefree, maintenance-free living where all responsibility for home care, recreation, or community activities are handled efficiently and promptly by others in return for a monthly fee. Others are seeking security, affordability, or some other objective. The wide variety of interests and spare time members may have leads to differing attitudes toward involvement in association affairs.

The challenge is to sustain a high level of awareness and support across the membership regardless of the degree to which each member may be actively involved in association. The board must acknowledge that a vitalized membership is the essential dynamic force without which a community cannot thrive.

Properly structured and implemented, the management strategy of an association promotes active involvement by those who are willing to serve on the board and active committees, while obtaining the enlightened support of those who are less involved. As active willing volunteers are recruited to help, the board then must determine what specific actions to take to develop and sustain community vitality. The first step is an assessment of how vital the association is.

There are a number of questions, which if answered will provide valid measures of effectiveness:

Are the members happy?

Is the association financially sound?

Are the members informed?

How do the property values of units within the association compare with previous prices or with those in neighboring communities?

What is the physical condition of the association's common property?

Is the crime rate rising? Is vandalism on the rise?

Are changes in the neighborhood a cause for concern?

Are the rules sound and are they generally willingly adhered to by the members.

Are there plans for the future? Are there adequate reserve funds for repair and replacement?

The way a community is governed sets the tone for the community as a whole. A very conservative board might ensure fiscal soundness but may lean toward liberal rule enforcement. Another board might have appropriated for a newly decorated clubhouse, but not adequately for roof or siding replacement. A weak board unable to make decision could well frustrate its members into apathy. A strong board acting in an autocratic manner could discourage participation, and lead its members to apathy. The realization of a revitalized community goal will depend in large measure upon the vitality, energy, and ability of community's volunteer force supporting committees.

Managers also play a vital part in the success of community programs. The method and procedures the professional manager uses to carry out the policies of the board will obviously have a significant effect on a community.

Keep the communications freely flowing in the community. If the board is unwilling to put out a newsletter because there are not enough volunteers, the manager should consider taking on this responsibility. The manager can suggest alternative methods of communications. Providing examples and materials from other communities.

Making and Acting on Motions

As outlined in Roberts' rules of order, parliamentary procedure requires that each item of business be brought before the board in the form of a motion. A motion is a formal proposal by a member on which the membership (or, at a board meeting, the board) must act.

Making a motion and acting on it requires seven steps:
(1) The member wishing to make a motion obtains the floor when formally recognized by the chair, thus gaining exclusive right to speak.
(2) The member makes a motion or proposal that is introduced by, "I move that…" and then the Motions follows. Long or complex Motions should be submitted in writing to the secretary prior to the meeting.
(3) The motion is then seconded by another member. The second to the motion indicates that at least one other member believes the subject to be important enough to be brought to discussion before the membership. If there is no second to the motion, it fails and cannot be discussed.
(4) The chair states the question, that is, he or she restates the motion, opening it to discussion. If a motion is not clear in its intent, the chair should put it in language that clarifies that intent. Before the question is stated, the maker of the motion may reword it or withdraw it entirely. Once the question has been stated, no changes may be made.
(5) The motion is open to discussion. The maker of the motion should be the first person to be called on. Each person wishing to speak

should be given one opportunity to do so. A second opportunity to speak may be awarded after everyone has had an opportunity to speak once. All discussions must be limited to the motion before the membership (or board).

(6) The chair puts the question to a vote by repeating the motion and calling for the vote on it. Most motions are passed by a simple majority of those votes present.

(7) The chair then announces the results of the vote, stating whether the motion has passed or failed.

Kinds of motions:

Most motions can be classified under four categories—main motions, subsidiary motions, privileged motions, and incidental motions. A main motion brings before the association members or board business that must be acted upon. The other types of motions, collectively called secondary motions, may relate to the main motion or to emergency or procedural questions.

Subsidiary Motions. A subsidiary motion changes or affects the way the main motion is handled, and must be voted on before the main motion is put to a vote. For example, a subsidiary motion to postpone indefinitely may occur when the main motion requires further study or more information, or is of questionable merit. When a motion is postponed indefinitely, the main motion is killed for the present and may not be given further consideration until the next meeting or a future meeting.

A member who wishes to modify a main motion in either its wording or by adding to it makes a motion to amend. An amendment to a motion only changes the wording of the original motion; it does not mean that the original motion is approved. When a motion is felt to have inadequate information, preventing reasonable debate or consideration, a motion is made to commit or refer it to a committee for study and resubmission at a later date. A motion to postpone definitely a decision on a pending question until a definite time serves to delay action on the pending questions until that time. This motion may also specify that date on which the question is to be recalled.

A problem common to many association meetings is debate that goes on indefinitely. To avoid this situation, a member may make a motion to limit debate. Such a motion may state a time limit for debate, or that it should end at a set time. It may also limit each speaker to a set amount of time for the debate. A motion may also be made to extend the limits of debate if the limits are too constrictive for an important topic. Another method of controlling time is to call the question—that is, bring it to an immediate vote.

The motion to lay on the table is one that is often abused or misused, as it permits temporarily setting aside a pending question in order to address more important matters. No specific time is set for re-addressing the question. A motion to table, although a necessary tool to enable the membership to deal with perhaps more important issues as they arise, should only be used to delay consideration of other questions, not to kill the pending question.

Privileged Motions.

A privileged motion relates to urgent or special matters and allows the interruption of other matters. As an example, a motion to call for the orders of the day requires conformance to the prescribed order of business and is made when the chair does not adhere to the agenda. A member also may make a motion to raise a question of privilege. This permits a member to interrupt pending business to state an urgent request or make a motion on an immediate problem, such as its being too noisy to hear the business being conducted.

A motion to recess proposes that a short intermission be called. It does not end the meeting and business is resumed after a recess at that point at which it was interrupted. A recess might be called to permit members time to count ballots, gather necessary information, hold informal consultations, or to recall a meeting due to failure to meet quorum requirements.

A motion to adjourn, which can be made and passed even while business is pending, proposes to end the meeting. The next meeting is scheduled before such adjournment, which may be done by a motion or a simple administrative solution.

Incidental Motions.

An incidental motion may involve a question of procedure that arises from another motion and must be considered before the motion in question is voted on. Most incidental motions are urgent and must be acted on immediately before business can proceed. Although numerous kinds of incidental motions may be made, there are five basic incidental motions.

A member who believes that the chair is not following parliamentary order may call attention to the fact by calling a point of order. The chair then rules on the point of order. If a point of order, or parliamentary rule, is to be intentionally violated, a motion to suspend the rules may be made. Where a member wishes that a main motion not be discussed, an objection to the consideration of the question is offered to prevent discussion of the motion. Such a motion may only be made before debate on the main motion has commenced and before any subsidiary motion has been stated.

If a pending main motion, or an amendment to it consists of two or more parts that may stand as individual questions, it can be moved to treat each part separately. This is a motion for division of the question. Discussion on a motion may be made either by voice vote or by a show of hands and the results are announced by the chair. If there is a question as to the chair's announcement of the vote, a member can demand a division of the assembly or a count.

Motions to Renew a Motion.

Robert's Rules of Order (which is essential for any association to own) provides a method by which motions that failed earlier Maybe brought up a second time. One such motion is a motion to take from the table, which reopens a motion tabled in a previous session. A motion to rescind cancels a previous action, while a motion to amend something previously adopted may be made to change the text or wording of a motion that already has been passed. This motion may be used only so long as the intent of the original motion is not changed.

While a question referred to committee is under study or review by the committee, no further motions to the question may be made. A motion to discharge a committee removes the question from the committee, returning it for vote. This parliamentary measure prevents unfair or unnecessary delay of a question by a committee.

When a motion already adopted is substantially reconsidered at the same meeting, a motion to reconsider must be made by a member who voted for the motion the first time. This action brings the question before the members or the board as though it had not been previously considered. Parliamentary procedure also prescribes that certain motions take precedence over certain other motions; that some motions need not be seconded; that some motions may not be amended, debated, or reconsidered; and that some motions require more than a simple majority vote.

Advice for Board Members

The members of the board, as elected leaders of the community, have an opportunity to set the tone of the community during their tenure.

1. Always post meeting notices regularly and on time. If possible, meetings should be scheduled at the same time each month (such as on the fourth Monday). A meeting toward the end of the month is preferable to having it in the first weeks because the property manager's report on delinquent accounts will be available for you.

2. Hold open board meetings and invite both owners and renters, which are ways of gaining the trust and support of the people living in the association, even if such meetings are sometimes a little inconvenient;

3. The board can often learn how the owners and renters genuinely feel about certain issues. Because of suggestions by owners for solving problems, the board can determine which owners among them will make good future board members.

4. Ask contractors and others such as the insurance agent to speak at board meetings. The grounds contractor, a tree specialist, even candidates running for the local school board are likely to be willing participants. This kind of participation is an excellent way to inform the members about matters that affect them.

5. Hold annual or biannual receptions to welcome all new owners, with all members of the board and officers present.

6. Make friends with the children in the association and, if possible, plan events for them, such as a summer picnic, a winter holiday party (perhaps with Santa Claus giving out inexpensive presents), an autumn tree walk or Halloween party in the clubhouse. Always ask the children to help organize the event and to be involved in its preparation.

7. Always be aware of the safety and well being of the owners and renters. If an emergency such as a fire arises, the owners and renters will cooperate amazingly well, if a calm firm president knows what to do.

8. Discourage name calling and arguments by owners at board meetings by remaining calm, listening carefully, but stating the facts regarding the issue firmly;

9. If it is anticipated that a owner appearing at a board meeting will be directing remarks at the president personally, ask the vice president or manager to preside at the meeting, thus allowing the president to remain silent, to listen carefully, and not to be drawn into heated controversy.

10. Award citations at the annual meeting to those owners and renters (exclusive of board members) who have contributed most to the effective operation of the association during the past year.

Rule Enforcement

Who enforces? Once (or perhaps before) a rule is adopted, enforcement of that rule obviously needs to be considered. If an association cannot or will not enforce a rule, it should not adopt it, for to do otherwise destroys administrative respect and effectiveness. Before violation of a rule is squarely presented to the board, a clear determination should be made as to who has the responsibility to enforce.

In a usual situation, rule enforcement is the ultimate responsibility of the board of directors. The manager's role in enforcement of a rule generally lies in its contract responsibilities, including advising of a violation, advising an owner of that violation and, ultimately, advising the owner of the actual fine imposed. This should be systematic, this should be the same for all unit owners. Please beware the board members themselves must be squeaky clean. What you do will be noticed!

It is not the manager who has the ultimate legal responsibility to enforce rules it is the BOD. Certainly, however, the manager, as well as association committees, can assist in rule enforcement. Aside from many other contractual responsibilities placed upon a manager, the manager is looked to by an association to help educate homeowners so that, hopefully, enforcement of rules is not necessary. This is an ongoing process and one which is not easily accomplished.

To further assist the board particularly in a large community, a rule enforcement committee structure should be considered. A committee to hear from the homeowner who is accused of a violation. This type of committee can set up a sort of judicial buffer between the violating homeowner and the board of directors. Such a "rules committee" or "covenants committee" or if you have a "architectural committee" the type of violation would determine which committee would hear the owner. The committee would receive copies of violations, from manager showing a copy of the notification sent to the alleged violator, as well as date required to comply or be heard by the committee when the fine would begin. The committee could not be the ultimate decision-making body for a sanction, the homeowner always has a right to come before the BOD. However it certainly would be proper for it to make a recommendation to begin the fine process if there was no response to a hearing option (which is the case most of the time.) If the owner still feels that a fine is not justified they must have an opportunity for a hearing with the BOD. At that point the Board will make a ruling to waive the fine or continue and seek legal means for violation compliance. Liens may be used when the fine reaches a certain level, to be determined by the BOD.

The developer's responsibility for rule enforcement should not be overlooked. In a normal situation, the developer controls the association by appointing members of the board of directors during the initial stages of the development. The same responsibilities which exist on homeowner board members for rule enforcement exist on the developer. In many situations, architectural changes, or standard house rules, are not as well regulated during the developer period control. However, failure of a developer to enforce rules pertaining to, for example, architectural changes, creates liability on the developer for failure to carry through with his fiduciary responsibilities as the developer controlled the first board of directors of the association. The developer's role is identical in rule enforcement and rule adoption to that of a homeowner board of directors.

Another entity to consider for rule enforcement is the individual homeowner. There are many cases where a complaint is made by a homeowner concerning another homeowner where the proper course of action of the association is merely to abstain and not use association funds(legal fees). An individual homeowner enforcement is appropriate when a "private" nuisance or action is taking place, as opposed to when a "public" nuisance or action in violation of the covenants exists. Excessive noise caused by one homeowner as an irritant to a second homeowner may well be a "private" nuisance with the association, children harassing another's child, one unit feud with another, a unit owner had a bike stolen and suspects that a particular person in the community did it. Deciding to abstain from involving itself in the controversy since the collective interests of the members is not involved.

Another example of this and one that worked very well for me, is the local government. The local township or city should not be overlooked. In many situations, a violation may also be the violation of a specific county, city or state code. What the association could seek is enforcement of its regulations through the administration of a township ordinance that is applicable to the situation. i.e. dogs running loose Without a leash, placing fencing, or other structures on common area which would otherwise need a permit from the township. This is not to say that the association would merely waive any rights to enforce its own regulations but, instead, what the association would be doing is turning in a formal complaint to the proper governmental department having jurisdiction over the matter and allowing that governmental department to evaluate and help bring this violation to a close.

Means of Rule Enforcement

Let's discuss rule enforcement further, as I stated previously, some rules and regulations are also local or state ordinances and that you can have the twp. or municipality get involved when you have a violation in the community that is also a local ordinance. I'll give you several examples, the community is zoned residential, no business may be operated out of unit. In the event you become aware of a violation of this rule, this would not only be a violation of your rules but also most probably of the residential use classification under the zoning ordinances.

In a homeowner situation it is not unusual that the association have regulations to limit the number of vehicles or prohibit parking of vehicles in the front yards or on other areas of the lot. Again here the zoning ordinances may assist in rule enforcement. The housing code, building code, and health code of local jurisdictions may well be applicable to rule violation situations. A building code usually would limit improvement to a unit unless a permit is first obtained. This helps with architectural violations. However, your community may have violations that are more stringent then the township. The local health code will limit the number of persons who may occupy a home. In better drafted health code ordinances not only will the state show a maximum number of people allowable in each unit but also a specified number of people that may occupy the square feet in a the home and the number of people by age and sex to live in specified number of bedrooms.

Ok.. let's move to how to enforce and how to minimize violations. Methods of rule violation avoidance will be labeled "preventive measures," while methods of rule violation sanctioning will be labeled "punitive measures."

(1)   Preventive measures. There are several miscellaneous measures by which an association might seek a greater degree of rule compliance. Newsletters, clearly drafted rules and regulations, rules handbooks with up to date amendments sent to all owners, and open board meetings.

A newsletter is an excellent means of keeping all homeowners informed. Informed homeowners are, in turn, more apt to understand how and why association policy has been formed, thus lessening discontent. A newsletter can also assist in seeking rule compliance by publication of a factual accounting of the events surrounding a past dispute or past actions which, if performed after the rule adoption, would be considered in violation of the rule.

Open board meetings are imperative. Closed board meetings can only result in the appearance of impropriety. Homeowner discontent, in turn, obviously leads to the increased chance of rules being violated.

A third measure to assist in seeking rule compliance is for the board of directors to draft clear rules and regulations when exercising the association's rule-making powers. This point can be illustrated by a condominium association which passed a rule regulating placement of screened doors. The rule stated that no formal approval need be obtained so long as the owner conformed to this guideline, "aluminum-framed storm doors or windows with aluminum finish could be placed on the front door." Without board approval, a homeowner placed a black aluminum screen door on his home. Immediately thereafter the homeowner received notices of violation of the rule. The BOD indicated that black would not be in conforming with the rule. They intended the door to be white aluminum. It seemed, that the board had initially contemplated "aluminum-framed storm windows with aluminum finish" to mean white or natural silver-like unfinished aluminum but did not specify that. Upon reflection, the board realized that the rule should have specified white. An unnecessary situation was created.

(2)   Punitive Measures. Obviously, attempts at preventing rule violation might not always be successful. While judicial recourse is always available for rule violation, experience has shown that there are many means by which a rule can be enforced without judicial recourse. Some of these measures are internal to the association; some are external, that is, involving a third party.

Internal Measures:

(a) **The Fining Power.** One means of punitive action after a rule is violated is for the association to fine its members. Under all circumstances, the fining power must be expressly incorporated into the association documents. The fining provision is effective in resolving enforcement of a rule. For example, where a junked up car is sitting on the property with 3 flat tires, without existence of the fining power, a community association would need to take this issue to court or use other means of enforcement. Instead, depending on your rules, you might be able to charge the owner $10.00 per day for every day the car is not moved out of site or repaired. Furthermore, cases concerning recreational vehicles illegally parked on the common areas are examples of situations where the fining power can assist in rule enforcement. With the fining power, the board can attempt to resolve these issues internally and if all other communications fail, *the fining* *power should not be indiscriminately or arbitrarily used but rather, in the proper case, complimented with a form of due process procedure.* The fining power should always be tied to an association's lien rights. The procedure would operate such that once a fine is levied, it is a lienable charge if not paid. In a suit on a lien, the association documents or condominium statutes should provide the association the right to collect legal fees.

(b) **Suspension of Rights and Assessment for Damages.** In addition to use of the fining power, the association should consider enforcement of a rule by means of suspension of voting and use rights. Additionally, assessments for physical damage may well be a means to enforce a regulation. The assessment for physical damage enforcement measure could be useful in several ways, including in a jurisdiction where the fining power might not be available. For example, the association may well determine that each time a dog excretes on the common area, damage in a certain amount is caused. That damage could be calculated by the clean-up costs associated with the violation. Many association documents give the board of directors the power to assess for this type physical damage or conduct which requires the association to perform certain maintenance. The charged amount if not paid will be placed as a lien after a certain approved amount has be accrued.

(c) **Self help.** In many jurisdictions the right of self-help for a violation of a regulation is permissible. Usually, an association document that allows such self-help will further specify that the association, its officers, and its agents, would not be liable for a trespass incurring during the violation, if a trespass is necessary. Along these same lines, some jurisdictions' case law establishes the right of self-help. This right has been established in cases where one person has placed their personal property on the real property of another. The owner of the real property then has the right to remove that personal property. This type judicial opinion clearly would establish the right of a homeowners association to remove an architectural violation on the common areas, since the common areas are owned by the homeowners association, and the architectural violation can be considered the personal property of the violator. Most of these cases, also, would require the association to avoid unnecessary damage to the personal property and imply that the association should take proper care of that personal property once removed.

(d) **Due Process.** Prior to the association instituting a fine for rule violation or exercising its adjudicative powers in any of the above ways, the association should adhere to some form of due process. The due process procedure can assist in rule enforcement by forcing face-to-face confrontations between the association and the violator, and by furnishing a forum to air grievances. In many cases, what superficially appears to be an irreconcilable controversy, deteriorates into a mere communication misunderstanding when the parties meet face-to-face. Before attempting rule enforcement by assessing a fine or by implementing such other enforcement measures, such as suspension of the right to vote, suspension of the use of community facilities like the pool you must give the alleged violator an opportunity to present his or her side to the BOD. Most importantly, not affording the violator the opportunity to be heard generally results in litigation to collect the fine or enforce the other measures. *Aside from the practical benefits of employing the due* *process procedure, increasingly, there is reason to believe such a procedure is, either by statute or judicial decision, legally required.* Surely this hearing should at least adhere to basic due process principles, such as notices and opportunity to be heard. *The Uniform Condominium Act (UCA), also requires a condominium association to afford a due process procedure before a fine can be imposed.* While courts have not yet directly considered the issue of whether a community association is required to follow due process procedures in exercising its adjudicative enforcement powers, it can be concluded that the judiciary in some jurisdictions, if confronted with the issue, would require adherence to due process.

This conclusion can be reached in light of the judicial view that community association rules are more similar to municipal by-laws than to private deed restrictions. The community association's imposition of a penalty for violation of a rule or covenant, therefore, is functionally equivalent to the imposition of a penalty by a municipality's judiciary for violation of an ordinance. In exercising the right of enforcement through adjudicative and enforcement powers under its declaration and, if applicable, the state condominium statute, the community association should be given the responsibility for observing due process. For practical and legal reasons, the association should adopt a standard of conduct for itself before internally enforcing a covenant or rule. For example, after receiving a complaint concerning certain actions of a unit owner, the association should notify the violator of the complaint and give him or her an opportunity to cure the situation. If the situation persists, the association should request a violator to appear at a hearing to be held by, perhaps, a covenants committee which consists of other members of the association and then the right to appeal to the members of the boards of directors. The opportunity to present his or her side of the issue should be given to the alleged violator at the hearing. At the same time, the complaining party or parties should be able to present their views. On the basis of what has been presented to the committee a sanction could be imposed. This is where the fining power can work quite successfully. Once determined that a violation has occurred and the sanction is imposed, the violator should have the additional opportunity to appeal this decision to the entire board of directors. The appeal hearing should then exclude any board members who sat on the initial hearing committee.

(e) External Measures. Aside from the potential for resolving association rule violations internally and hopefully preventing litigation, community associations may wish to consider external means of rule enforcement, short of litigation. While two types of external measures are apparent, neither are presently being extensively used. One such measure is provided where a state sets up an arbitration-type process. The process basically involves an advisory board to review issues concerning disputes between a unit owner and the association or a management decision. Secondly, there is a program under the auspices of the American Arbitration Association's Dispute Service and has been established to divert minor disputes, in situations other than community associations, away from the courts. The prime purpose of a privately established mechanism for mediation is to reach an agreement with which both sides are comfortable. Certainly, this is not to suggest that the community association should be looking for a means to compromise rule enforcement; however, there are many gray areas involved in rule enforcement and in selected cases mediation may well be appropriate. In some type situations, mediation would seem completely foreign to association rule enforcement. For example, in architectural violation cases the courts have already established that the aesthetic judgment of anyone other than the board of directors is usually irrelevant to the decision. In these type situations, therefore, the association's elected officials are the proper parties to exercise their sound business discretion.

Collection of Assessments

The first step regarding assessment collection and for that matter any procedure developed by the board is to first REVIEW THE GOVERNING DOCUMENTS. They may establish the guidelines. When the board is establishing additional guidelines, this should not be done in a vacuum. Consult your manager or managing agent as well as the association attorney. If the documents do not provide or is silent on specific guidelines then the BOD must adopt formal guidelines that must be followed in ALL cases of delinquent assessment. This does not mean that in certain cases of extreme hardship a payment agreement cannot be worked out. **That is always the first choice.** THE FIRST STEP IS TO DETERMINE WHEN THE FEE IS ACTUALLY DELINQUENT. 10 days after the due date, 15, 20? Then as soon as the payment is "delinquent" a reminder notice should be mailed to the unit owner. Then if the payment is not received by the second period of time, as determined by the board, a certified and /or hand delivered letter reminding the unit owner of their obligation to pay is sent and gives the owner a specified number of days in which to pay or legal action will be taken.

The specific legal action is outlined in your governing documents. There may be additional guidelines that are established by the BOD. The guidelines are followed by the managing agent or manager of your community. This involves late notices and late penalty charges, voting restrictions, use restrictions, judgement and lien. The managing agent or manager should know the extent of their authority with regards to follow through of these guidelines. Generally their role extends through notices, fines, self help use restrictions and then the BOD gives the final word on liens. Through frequent board meetings and review of the delinquent accounts the BOD is kept up to date on the steps taken on delinquent owners. The BOD should review with the manager or managing agent the routine steps followed with the delinquent accounts and if necessary revision should be made by the BOD.

Assessment Collection Procedure

THIS IS A SAMPLE COLLECTION PROCEDURE:

THIS IS A SUGGESTED PROCEDURE. THIS PROCEDURE MUST BE COMPARED WITH YOUR GOVERNING DOCUMENTS AND THEN REVIEWED BY YOUR ATTORNEY BEFORE IT IS IMPLEMENTED.

Or as I prefer to call it {scream}(*show me the money*) from the film Jerry McQuire.)

ASSESSMENT COLLECTION PROCEDURE

1. Initial Billings.

All billings for monthly installments of Annual Assessments shall be placed in the mail in the beginning of the forth week of each month. Each billing will indicate:

A. The amount and due date of the current installment.

B. Amount of any unpaid assessments and any late charges, fines etc. from previous billings. The due date shall be the first day of the month following the month in which the billings are mailed . Upon receipt of the check from each member, the treasurer, property manager or designee, shall enter in the books of the association the bank name, address and account number of that member.

2. Notice of Delinquency.

A first notice of delinquency shall be mailed on or about the 15th of the month. The letter should explain various recourses the association has available to it for collection and indicate the late charge that has been placed on their account.

Phone numbers shall be given if there are any questions involving the bill.

The treasurer or the manager shall continue following this procedure for assessment collection, until otherwise directed by the board.

3. Acceleration Notice- Second notice

The acceleration notice should be mailed certified, return receipt requested on or about 30 days in arrears. This notice is mailed to each member unless there are extenuating circumstances determined by the board. The notice to accelerate shall state that (1) the board intends to accelerate the balance of the installments of the annual assessment for the fiscal year and (2) a lien is about to be placed on the member's property for the full amount of the annual assessment and other charges, unless full payment of all past-due assessments and late charges is received within thirty (30) days of the date of this notice

4. Phone Call. (optional)

An attempt to reach the defaulting member by telephone will be made within ten (10) days after mailing the formal second notice of acceleration and before any legal proceedings are started.

5. Third Notice or Legal Demand Letter.

The treasurer or the manager may authorize the attorneys to prepare and mail a final demand letter to the defaulting member, advising the member that legal action in the form of a lien will commence if the delinquent assessment and other charges are not paid within fifteen (15) days following the date of this mailing. 6.. **Recording of Notice of Assessment (Lien).**

The treasurer or the manager will record the notice of assessment (lien)in the office of the County Records. The notice of assessment will be recorded no sooner than thirty (30) days after the date of postmark of the acceleration final notice unless there are extenuating circumstances as determined by the board.

(a) A letter shall be sent to a unit owner as soon as the notice of assessment(lien) has been recorded. Telling him or her that the board has elected to accelerate the annual assessment.

(b) A lien has been filed against his or her condominium and

(c) The association intends to retain legal counsel, at the cost of the member, to enforce the collection of the assessments and other charges, unless all delinquent assessments and other accrued charges are paid in full immediately.

(d) A copy of the acceleration notice shall be mailed to each first mortgagee of a mortgage on the condominium of a defaulting member.

7. Legal Action.

After consulting with legal counsel, the board may direct the association's attorney to commence a lawsuit for money at least thirty (30) days following the date of the attorney's demand letter, or to commence any other action authorized by law and the declaration of covenants, conditions and restrictions, including judicial foreclosure of the assessment lien or foreclosure. **Only the board, by resolution, may authorize the attorneys to actually commence any lawsuit to collect past-due assessments.** Be sure to check your state laws involving the option of foreclosure,

(it is difficult action, costly and one that is rarely taken.) Foreclosure involves private power of sale, as stipulated in item #8, following a resolution by the board authorizing such action. Normally the association does not take this extreme action. We just impose a lien with the knowledge that when the owner sells the unit your lien will get paid. When there is a sale on the unit you *should* get your money.

It should be noted that there are times when liens are not detected before a sale, that is why it is important that **when you become aware of a sale you must make sure the realtor or new owners are** notified of any liens. The board shall be informed of all judgments obtained, and no enforcement of any judgment obtained shall take place without board approval. Because unsuccessful plaintiffs have no right of appeal from adverse judgments in small claims court, and because homeowner associations have fared poorly in small claims court, it is usually recommended that assessment collection lawsuits be filed by the association in municipal or superior Court.

8. Enforcement of Municipal or Superior Court Judgment.

Unless instructed otherwise by the board, if a municipal or superior court judgment is obtained, the association's attorney or the manager shall send a final demand letter to the defaulting member ("defendant"), together with a copy of the judgment, within ten (10) days following the date of the judgment. The final letter shall inform the defendant that the association intends to obtain a writ of execution and to levy through the local sheriff upon any personal property owned by the defendant which is located in the County. Ten (10) days after the date of that final notice the attorney for the association or the manager, as the case may be, shall obtain a writ of execution from the court and shall thereafter complete sheriff's instructions authorizing and directing the sheriff to seize certain listed personal property owned by the defendant. Legal counsel must be obtained for the enforcement procedure in this paragraph.

9. Extension of Lien.

If all amounts reflected on the notice of assessment have not been paid in full within one (1) year from the date on which the notice is recorded, or if enforcement of the lien (either by private power of sale or by suit for judicial foreclosure) has not been initiated within such one (1) year period, then an extension of lien shall be recorded by the attorney or the manager in the office of the county recorder. A copy of the recorded extension should be sent to the member and to his or her listed mortgagees, when it is received from the recorder. **To protect the rights of the association, an extension of lien should be filed even if a lawsuit for money has been commenced within such one (1) year period.**

10. Release of Lien.

When all amounts stated in the notice of assessment and all other charges and costs which may have then accrued have been fully paid, a release of lien shall be recorded by the attorney or the manager in the office of the county recorder. The treasurer or the manager shall send to the "reinstated" member a letter of reinstatement, together with a copy of the recorded release of lien .

11. Certificate of Assessment.

Upon written request, a certificate in writing signed by the president of the BOD or the manager on behalf of the association shall be furnished to any interested party, which certificate shall set forth the amount of the annual assessment of the specified condominium unit, the due dates of the installments and whether there are any monies due or violations pending involving that unit i.e. architectural control issues.

12. Letter of Introduction.

As soon as the board becomes aware of any sale of a condominium in that community, the manager or president of the board shall promptly mail a letter of introduction to the new owner welcoming him or her as a new member of the association. This letter shall briefly outline the responsibilities of the board and the new member, including the obligation to pay assessments to the association. The letter shall accompany a copy of the POS containing the articles of incorporation, bylaws, a copy of the recorded declaration, current budget and a up to date rules handbook. It will be wise to have a form for them to sign and return indicating receipt of the materials. On that form you might have them supply some phone numbers in the event of an emergency as well. This signed receipt is particularly important in any future issues involving receipt of the rules and regulations.

The Budget

Remember when I told you one of the most important things you must have as a board member was a sense of humor? Well, this topic is the hardest to fine the humor in....the budget process! Now the budget is a guideline of anticipated expenses and estimated income for any given time. For an Association most typically a one year period. The first budget for a community is completed by the developer prior to any owners and is in the (POS) Public Offering statement booklet containing the governing documents of the community. Yes, it is my experience that the majority of budgets completed by the developer is low. The first budget after the unit owners take control can be very unpopular because of a substantial increase. Now your manager or managing agent is generally responsible for preparation of a proposed budget. Some communities have special committees just for this purpose. With, as I recommend for every committee, one member of the BOD on that committee. It is preferable that the individuals that work on this committee have some background in the job at hand. In the case of a budget committee an accountant, bookkeeper, banker, or an individual familiar with budgets if at all possible. Try to tap into those resources in the community.

I developed a narrative many years ago that explained, in detail each line item for the BOD. They could easily see what was included in the item and what was not. It listed specifically what was appropriated for the year on certain items and what would have to wait until next year. I felt this worked so successfully that it should extend beyond just a companion to the budget for the BOD but also to all the membership. I know…I know..boards generally feel that to much information can create more problems in the end or that owners cannot comprehend and will get lost with all the wording but..I disagree. My experience tells me different.

There is no question that a lot of residents will not even read or want to read the narrative or budget…they are just the bottom line. To help those who are trying to understand, the narrative must be very simply stated, and easily read. I realize it is difficult for people who are not use to reading budgets to read them but try to write as elementary and simple as possible about each line item in the budget. For instance show what is included with lawn care. Owners see that giant number and think something is not kosher. They have no idea all the work that is included in that category.. Be specific about the number of cuts and type and number of chemicals and what they are used to treat and when in the season they will be applied, any other work approved during the year, edging, weed control, sprinkler system maintenance, shrub and tree replacement, aeration, lime and fertilizer applications, reseeding, mulch and seasonal flowers when and where they will be planted, around the tennis court and entrances in spring, summer and fall etc. Be very specific. The narrative is a lot of work..a lot of work…but the most work is the first year you do it. Then year after year you just refine and adjust it. The hardest is individualizing each line item the first time. Take electric for instance, what are you paying electricity on? The clubhouse, all the common lighting, entrance and parking lot lights, flood lights on all buildings, utilities for clubhouse and office, aerator pump in lake. You break down each line item and what is included in it. Talk to your manager or managing agent about a narrative to accompany the budget. Creating a budget is very time consuming. That is why it is imperative that a time table be set to begin preparation. If your fiscal year begins in January and you want to approve a budget in November to be distributed in December. You had better start in the summer gathering bids and information. Please be sure to check your documents to be sure of the amount of time required for unit owners to receive the proposed budget. Beginning preparation in the summer is very common.

You can present the proposed budget to the BOD in October with possible revisions to be completed for the November Board meeting for final approval. In budget preparation you want to get feedback from the various committees on their needs, if any. Remind all committees to present anticipated expenses for the coming year. If you remember we talked about the newsletter committee and the regular monthly expenses for printing, mailing paper products, camera film, computer software. It is the time to get new bids..i.e. on printing and come up with alternatives to spending some of money…to evaluate the expenses from last year.

It is important when evaluating a change of service that you give the same specs to every company. Sometimes you will get a low bid and wonder why one company can do the same work, assuming you have given all the same specs. The reason is they might not have insurance, painting contractors are the ones I've encountered the most in this area. Their expenses are more if they carry insurance so they charge more. I must stress to all board members, if you have a contractors that has done everything to please and you are happy with their work do not sell them out for a few bucks! The most I've encountered in this area are landscapers. It is very hard to get reliable, responsible landscapers. Every year we go to the drawing board and have specs that are the same and another landscaper comes in a few hundred dollars lower. If you are not happy with your current service and checked references, which you should always do, then go for the new one. If not, don't do it, chances are the next year they will bump up the charges because they "underestimated the job". You don't want the reputation that you change contractor no matter what every year. Use good business sense, if you are pleased, I can't stress this enough *your integrity is important.* **Don't sell out for a couple of bucks if someone busted their butt for you all year or for even several years.**

You need to have this information when preparing the first draft of the budget, streamlining wherever possible. So time factors for their response is very important and it is my experience that committees need more then one reminder that you are waiting for their input. The budget timetable should allow for an open public meetings of the membership so the unit owners can voice their opinions and have their questions answered about the budget.

As part of its obligation to preserve and protect the common areas, the association must be prepared for expected and emergency repairs and replacements. We can calculate the expected but with regards to emergencies, it is generally accepted that 3% to 5% of your annual income be placed in a contingency fund for unforeseen emergencies.

The Uniform Condominium Act as well as most governing documents require that the BOD maintain reasonable reserves for major replacements. Eventually every condominium will need major repairs and replacements. Establishing reserves minimizes the risk that owners will encounter large special assessments. Some specific reserve items of expected replacements, roofing, siding, deck/wood replacement, sidewalks, parking lot paving, clubhouse a/c and heating replacement, tennis court resurfacing, roadway repaving.

For estimated reserve funds needed you must have a professional in that area or an engineer who specializes in reserve studies, access the condition of the item and give an estimated life expectancy and replace-ment cost value on the item. As an example ..it is determined that there is a 5 years life remaining on the siding of the clubhouse. Estimated cost of on repair/replacement is $5000 you need to allocate $1000 per year for 5 years to be prepared for that work. You don't want to divide the cost in a special assessment...so be prepared and bite the bullet now. Professional managers and managing companies usually do there homework and should know the standard guide for each item.

11/31/2000

Happiness Condominium Association

2001 BUDGET NARRATIVE

CONDOMINIUM ASSESSMENTS are determined each year after extensive study and evaluation by the association board members and management. These are the funds required to cover the daily operations of the association as well as capital replacement/reserve items. Disbursements from the operating account including payments for all services, labor, materials, supplies for annual repairs as well as operating expenses for the grounds. Reserves for future repairs such as roofs and driveways are collected and placed in savings accounts or certificates of deposit.

Total Condominium Assessments are: $

The distribution between operating and reserve accounts this year will be $ for Operations and $ for Reserves for an increase of $ or % This increase from last year's budget is necessary to continue operations at there current level so that we will adequately maintain the property on an annual basis, given the projected increase of cost in the new fiscal year.

4400 INTEREST INCOME will be earned upon the reserve accounts and upon temporarily invested surplus operating cash. This interest is computed using an estimated reserve account average balance of $350,000; $320,000 of which is invested in Certificates of Deposit yielding greater than 8% interest and a reserve savings account of $30,000 for emergency needs. This interest varies but should average 5.50%.

Total Reserve Interest is: $

There will be an average monthly carryover of $15,000 in the operating account which earns interest at 5.25% and will add an estimated $790 in earnings.

Total Operating Interest is: $

Interest is recorded monthly for each savings account or Certificate of Deposit.

Total Projected Interest: $

4700 MISCELLANEOUS INCOME represents assessments for late fees of $ (assessed at a rate of $15 for all payments not received by the 10th of the month), and rule violation fines, clubhouse and pool rental fees.

Total Miscellaneous Income is: $
TOTAL CASH RECEIPTS ARE: $
EXPENSES: $
ADMINISTRATIVE EXPENSES: $

5000 ASSOCIATION misc. functions is a term for community functions such as social functions $750, board meetings $200, education for board members $250 and items of recognition for services to the community $50.

Total Misc. functions is: $

5100 INCOME TAXES—The association is required to file an annual tax return, normally at the non profit status. Each year the association's accountants will determine the relative merits of each filing possibility and file under the format with the least tax liability. It is anticipated that we will file as a non profit corporation in 2001The 2000 tax liability, payable in 2001, is projected to be $

All prior years' tax returns have been filed and there is no unpaid tax liability.

5200 INSURANCE—Article XI of the HAPPINESS Condominium Association Declaration states: "The board shall obtain and at all times maintain insurance against loss, damage to or destruction of the common Elements and limited common elements by fire and such other risks as may be covered under standard extended coverage provisions to the extent of the **full replacement cost thereof**, with such deductible as the Board may determine, and shall obtain and maintain insurance against loss damage to or destruction of the Units by fire and such other risks as may be covered under standard extended coverage provisions to the extent of all or any part of the **full replacement cost thereof**." All insurance affecting the property shall be governed by the provisions of this section. In compliance with this provision, the board has arranged for insurance as required by the legal documents and recommended by their insurance agent.

The Insurance Carrier for Happiness is: Traveler's Insurance HAPPINESS is insured for approximately $ in buildings and contents for association-owned items including maintenance equipment.

ONLY CONDOMINIUM PROPERTY IN COMMON AND LIMITED COMMON PROPERTY IS COVERED BY THE MASTER POLICY. OWNERS MUST HAVE INDIVIDUAL COVERAGE UNDER A HOMEOWNER POLICY FOR YOUR OWNED CONTENTS, IMPROVEMENTS, BETTERMENT AND LIABILITY. PLEASE CONTACT YOUR INSURANCE AGENT TO DETERMINE IF YOU ARE PROPERLY INSURED. IF YOU RENT YOUR UNIT, YOU MUST REQUIRE YOUR TENANT TO SECURE PROPER INSURANCE ON THEIR PROPERTY OR YOU AS THE OWNER COULD BE LIABLE FOR THEIR LOSS.

1) Master Association Policy:
    This is primarily designed to replace or repair buildings in the event of a fire or other covered loss. Current insurance carrier is the Travelers Insurance Company under policy number 650-492J354-9TIA-2000.
    Your policy is set at 100% of replacement cost and the Association has a $1,000 deductible per occurrence. You as an individual may be required to pay part or all of this deductible if your individual unit property is damaged and is covered by the Master Policy. Be sure your individual policy has the proper wording to cover your portion of any deductible assessed against you.
    This current policy is effective until January 15, 2001 and will be renewed on that date. The annual premium is expected to be $ payable in quarterly installments.

2) Liability Insurance:
    This coverage is designed to protect the association, all officers of the association and managing agents of the association against claims of anyone suffering injury on the grounds owned by the association. The coverage will also pay for the legal defense of the association even when no damage claims are successful. This coverage is included in the Master Policy premium.

3) Directors and Officers Insurance: $
    Serving on the Board of Directors of the HAPPINESS Condominium Association are elected unit owners. This position is an unpaid community service that entails considerable work and is a volunteer effort. The Board is ultimately responsible for the operation of the association and all the decisions made in its operation. In order to protect the serving board, the association secures this insurance to defend board members against claims made for decisions and actions arising as a result of board membership. The amount of coverage is $1,000,000

and is included in the master policy. **Be sure the committee members ad hoc or permanent are covered as well.**

4)   Catastrophe Umbrella Policy:
     This covers the association for an additional $1,000,000 of supplemental insurance, over and above the basic liability coverage as stipulated in item 2. The premium is expected to $

5)   Comprehensive Automobile Liability:
     This policy covers the association for bodily injury and property damage caused by the association truck used by an association employee or volunteer while on association business. The premium is estimated to be $ and the policy period is to February 1, 2001.

6)   Fidelity Coverage:
     This coverage in the amount of $ protects the Association from theft of funds by employees and board Members as well as the management company employees who have access to association funds. The anticipated premium is $

Total Insurance Expenses: $

5300 OFFICE SERVICES by the management agent are performed on behalf of the association and billed to the association at set rates. According to contract. Telephone costs, extra on site time, extra board or committee meetings other additional administrative support included in this line item. The charge for copies has been reduced this year from $.12 cents to $.10 cents per copy, however, usage has remained high with the desire to send mailings and supportive information to the residents. Copy costs for 2001, based on actual usage from 2000, are budgeted to be $.

Total additional Office Services are:$

5400 OFFICE SUPPLIES are those items supplied by the management company for the association and billed to the association at set rates. Such items as postage, new rules distribution, stationery, payment envelopes, late charge slips newsletter distribution to absentee owners, payment coupons, supplies for all office equipment and other specific items used exclusively for HAPPINESS are included in this line item.

Total Office Supplies are: $

5500 PROFESSIONAL SERVICES:

5510 ACCOUNTING: The Code of Regulations of HAPPINESS requires that the treasurer of the association maintain accurate association books and records. The records are submitted for an audit annually by an independent CPA. As required by the documents. This audit is to assure that association that funds have been properly accounted for.

Management contract includes site inspections Monday, Wednesday and Friday 1pm -3pm and 10 board meetings per year (specify contractual obligations. Meet with Landscape committee once a month, specify time, attend and advise architectural hearings, prepare agenda, send late notices, handle calls from owners all week or just on the days noted, show contract in this area.

REALGOOD PROPERTY MANAGEMENT Inc.

1000 Nocomplaints Boulevard, North

Anywhere, PA 15205

(666) 123-4567

Attn: Kathleen Dontcallme

Total Management Service contract: $

5590   LEGAL FEES:

It is anticipated that legal fees including retainer which is $500.00, cost of appearance at four(4) board meetings per year including the annual budget meeting and any consultations will be $2500.

5800 EMPLOYEE EXPENSES:

PERMANENT STAFF WAGES:

A) One maintenance supervisor is employed full-time. The supervisor current salary is $ In the year 2000 projected for a 15% increase which will bring his salary to a more competed rate of $ there will be a holiday bonus of $500, which is an increase of $100.00 from the previous year. Additional benefits include a two-week paid vacation, a life insurance policy for $10,000, and six paid holidays. This compensation package is competitive with industry standards and allows Happiness to attract and retain qualified employees.

B) A Maintenance Assistant will be employed full-time, forty (40) hours per week. This employee will be paid at a rate of $ per hour for the year 2000. A 12% increase from the previous year. There will be a holiday bonus of $250. which is an increase of $50.00 from the previous year. Additional benefits include a one-week paid vacation, a life insurance policy for $5000 and six paid holidays. This compensation package is competitive with industry standards and allows Happiness to attract and retain qualified employees. provision has been made for a holiday bonus of $250. Medical benefits for two permanent staff members include AETNA US HEALTHCARE HMO coverage.

Summary of Permanent Staff Compensation:

A) Maintenance Supervisor. B) Maintenance Assistant.

	A.	B.
Wages	$	$
Bonus	$	$
USHC $	$	
Life Insurance	$	$
Disability Ins.	$	$
Uniforms	$	$
Worker's Comp.	$	$
Total Comp. Package		$
Total Permanent Staff Wages:		$

5900 SEASONAL STAFF WAGES: HAPPINESS residents take great pride in the appearance of the grounds. It is the board's desire to continue to maintain and improve the buildings and grounds with high standards. Painting services will be done in house during the spring and summer.

A) Two grounds attendants employed 18 weeks each. Picking up from the grounds, sweeping around dumpster and or trash collection areas. Sweeping tennis courts and basketball courts. Cleaning playground area and around the pools. The pay rate will be $6.50 per hour for 1st year staff and $7.50 per hour for returning staff. We anticipate that we will hire one new and one returning attendant.

B) Three lifeguard positions for 16 weeks. The pool will be open 12pm to 8pm Monday thru Friday and 10 to 5 Saturday and Sunday. The pool will open the Saturday of memorial day weekend and close the Sunday of labor day weekend. The pay rate is $6.50 per hour for 1st year and $7.50 per hour for returning staff.

C) Casual Labor: One laborer will work full-time during the summer season and assist the permanent staff on a part-time basis during the rest of the year. The planned schedule for 2001 is forty (40) hours per week starting June 1 and through September 15 and then two (2) days per week (16 hours) the rest of the year. This person will be a contract laborer at a rate of $7.50 per hour and will help our maintenance staff with painting and refurbishing the property after the winter. Painting clubhouse, repairing play areas, painting fences around the dumpster areas, painting fencing around some of the perimeter areas of the community and other jobs associated with a spring clean up and repair. This person's time will be allocated to provide the service necessary during the peak work period.

Summary of Seasonal Staff Compensation: $

A)2 Grounds Attendants B) 3 Lifeguards C) Casual Labor
$ $ $

6000 EMPLOYER PAYROLL TAXES: We pay all employees on a semi-monthly basis. The maintenance supervisor reports all normal hours and authorized overtime, to the management office's accounting department according to the payroll cut off schedule. After processing, the checks are delivered to the employees the second working day thereafter.

Holiday bonuses are paid, upon final authorization of the board, in December of each year.

FICA (Federal Insurance Contribution Act)-This rate is determined by the Social Security Administration.

FUTA (Federal Unemployment Compensation)-This payroll tax is determined annually by the U.S. Department of Labor. The 2001 rate is expected to remain % of the first $ of gross pay per employee.

SUI Each employer's rate is set by the (state) unemployment department according to there requirement.

Payroll Tax Recapitulation:
FICA   FUTA SUI   TOTAL

6012 BENEFITS: MEDICAL—The maintenance supervisor and assistant Supervisor receive paid medical insurance based on single coverage. If the employee desires additional coverage, the extra cost is paid by the employee through a payroll deduction. The current provider AETNA US HEALTHCARE HMO. The current rate for the single plan is approximately $140 per month through June, 2000, and $ per month from July, 2000, through the end of the year.

Total Medical Insurance Expense: $

LIFE INSURANCE in the amount of $10,000 for each full-time staff member is provided under a company group plan after one year of service. The premium is approximately $ per employee.

Total Life Insurance $ per month

DISABILITY INSURANCE PROGRAMS—These programs provide protection for both the Association and the employee. This coverage will pay the employee 66% of their salary up to age 65 for a non-job related injury or illness. There is a one week waiting period before the coverage takes effect. The premium for this insurance is based on the employee's salary.

Total Disability Insurance $

UNIFORMS—A professional maintenance staff is more readily identifiable and present a heater appearance for the community when uniformly attired. Therefore, we issue all permanent staff members uniforms. There is an allocation of $200 for an annual uniform allowance per permanent employees for replacement uniforms. Seasonal staff will be issued tee-shirts and be required to purchase work boots at their expense. The laundering and care of the company issued uniforms will be the responsibility of each employee.

Total Uniform Expense: $

WORKER'S COMPENSATION INSURANCE—This coverage compensates a worker who is injured on the job for medical as well as lost wage claims. The rates for this coverage are set by the state and currently are assessed as a percentage of the wages paid and rates vary according to the state classification rating for each labor category.

Position	Rate as %	Est. Annual
Maintenance	%	
Grounds	%	
Lifeguards	%	
Total Benefits:	$ 8,455	

TOTAL EMPLOYEE EXPENSES:$ 76,680

6300 MAINTENANCE EXPENSES:

COMMON BUILDINGS/ROOMS is the area where all expenses for the community and maintenance building are calculated. This year's budget of $400 is a $200 reduction from the prior year and the allocation is for minor repairs. Interior will be painted in house in the spring.

   Total Community Buildings $

6400 CLEANING SUPPLIES is a budget line for soap, brooms, wax, paper towels, toilet paper, brushes, sponges, disinfectants, etc. that are used at the pool, community room and for maintenance operations.

   Total Cleaning Supplies are: $

6450 CONCRETE REPAIRS is for the repair to or replacement of curbs, sidewalks, steps, patios, etc. We anticipate only minor repairs in this area specifically on the area across from units # 10 and 15

   Total Concrete Repairs are: $

6500 EQUIPMENT includes the purchase, operation, repair or rental of all power driven equipment and tools. Non-power hand tools are also included in this heading. Within the section entitled operation are such expendable items as gas, oil and lubricants. The budget for this is as follows:

   6510   Operation: Gas & oil for the truck, routine maintenance, oil change, tune up, two new tires are needed and winterizing.
          Other purchases, Chain saw $
   6540   Repairs: $
          Hand leaf blower, misc. equipment, based on averages from prior years.
          Small Tools: $
          Misc. hand tool purchases
   Total Equipment Expenses: $

6600 EXTERIOR BUILDING REPAIR represents all common repairs and maintenance to the residential buildings, from the roofs and gutters to the foundations. All expenses related to the common elements of residential buildings will be included in this line item.

10 Balconies units 1–10 $
replacement of approximately_unit numbers
70–2"x 6"x 16';20—2"x 6"x 12';
15 -2"x 10"x 16' (spindles)
50 -4"x 4"x 8'; 15 -2"x 4"x 10' with
treated lumber
Door Frames: $ 1,200
two sets of side lights and floods in lot by buildings #15 and #17
Gutters/Downspouts/Repair and cleaning $ 200
Total Exterior Building Repairs: $

6800 Grounds Expense includes expenses for all common ground,
ground cover, shrubs, fences and water drainage.
26 lawn cuttings, edging and weed eater at each cut $ Total $
reseeding lawns: buildings 1 thru 12: $20 per yard
2 applications of fertilizer spring and fall & weed control- $ reseed
area across from lake $ lime in fall aeration, dethatching area near
buildings 25 and 27 $
30 Shrubs $ around tennis court misc. lawn care $
240 yds. shredded mulch $ per square yard totals $ for all scrub and
trees within the community.
decorative large rocks$ 3000 at entrance
2 professional shrub trimmings spring and fall $
6 deciduous trees ($200) $ 1,200
30 replacement trees $ 2,800
55 new pine trees in area by clubhouse and tennis court $ ground
cover for common area on hillside across unit 19 $ 3,850
insect/disease spray $ 1,500
flowers $ 1000 at entrance spring and fall only install one french
drain by play area in section 10 $
Total Grounds: $

7000 MAINTENANCE SUPPLIES:

PAINTING includes the allocation for power washing and staining of fences around the dumpster areas. In addition this year's budget is based on a schedule to stain 25 decks in section one(in the order in which they were built as determined through field inspection, plus miscellaneous spot painting in various areas in the community.

Contractors will be painting all unit decks. The on-site staff will stain privacy fences. The association will purchase the paint and stain for the contractor. The material cost for all painting includes:

Paint	$ 2,890
110 gal. @ $19 each	$
50 gal. stain @ $16 each	$
25 gal. stain @ $10 each	$
in 5 gal cans	
Misc. painting supplies $	

Contractors will paint doors and window trim of section one of the community this year and section two next year.

55 units at an average cost of $280 per unit for labor and 25 decks at $190 each. Total cost for the contracts is expected to be $20,150. We have increased the number of units to be painted by the contractors to provide for an earlier completion of the program and to eliminate the difficulty we have experienced in prior year's to secure sufficient qualified summer employees for this skilled task.

Total Painting Expenses: $

7100 RECREATIONAL FACILITIES include all expenses for the picnic area, playground, swimming pool and tennis courts.

7710 swimming pool $
furnishings (1 small table & 4 lounge chairs replacements)

7720   pool operation $
Chemicals (list) $

7880 Recreational facilities

tennis courts $

Color coat the entire surface from reserves contracted $

Total Recreational Facilities $

7200 ROADS/PARKS/DRIVEWAYS represents the cost of repairing, sealing and resurfacing the parking areas in section one on Howdy Drive. This year's budget amount of $4,000 is to continue to seal the driveways. The plan is to seal 70 driveways at a cost of $55 each. We have allowed for $150 for extra expenses.

Total Roads/Parking/Driveways: $

7300 UTILITY REPAIRS represents an allotment for light bulbs, small repair parts for flood lights and parking lot lighting and including tennis court lights, electrical, heating and plumbing equipment on the property.

Total Utility Repairs are: $

7410 SNOW REMOVAL is the estimated cost for all supplies necessary for the on-site staff to help clear walkways and steps.

200 80# bags rock salt @ $3 $ 600

40 50# bags calcium @ $10 $ 400

4 snow shovels @ $10 $ 40

10 pairs of gloves @ $5 $ 50

Snow removal contract estimated cost $5,000 based upon an average of last three year's figures.

Total Snow Removal Expenses: $

7420 RUBBISH REMOVAL is for trash removal from units on a weekly basis and residential dumpsters provided as needed. The budgeted amount has not increased. The refuse company that services HAPPINESS Valley Refuse

Total Rubbish Removal: $

7450 EXTERMINATING costs for this year is comprised of material costs to remove bees and insects by the on-site staff as necessary, common areas only. Renewal of 5 year termite maintenance agreements for buildings A through H

Total Exterminating Expense: $

7500 MISCELLANEOUS MAINTENANCE is for various small maintenance repairs and expenses that do not fit into another category.

Total Misc. Maintenance Expenses: $

TOTAL MAINTENANCE EXPENSES $

7600 UTILITY EXPENSES: These are based on actual costs from 2000 and for common areas only.

7610 ELECTRIC represents all street lights, flood lights on buildings, maintenance shop, community building, tennis court lighting and pool operation. This budget reflects a 10% increase in rates. The electric company that services HAPPINESS is:

Bright Light Company
Box 100w
Pittsburgh, PA 15230

Total Electric Expense is: $

7620 GAS is for heating of the clubhouse ad offices maintenance buildings This year's budget does not reflect an increase in costs. The gas company that services HAPPINESS is:

WEHAVE GAS COMPANY
P.O. Box 371304-MMM
Pittsburgh, PA 15250-7304

Total Gas Expense is: $

7630 WATER is used for all pool and maintenance operations. This budget contains an increase of $100 based on actual billings for 2000. The water company that services HAPPINESS is:

HOLDYOURWATER COMPANY
410 DRIP LANE
Pittsburgh, PA 15234-1111
Total Water Expense: $

7640 SEWAGE is projected at approximately two-thirds of the cost of water.
Total Sewage Expense: $
TOTAL UTILITY EXPENSES: $
OTHER EXPENSES:

7705 CAPITAL IMPROVEMENTS
None are scheduled for this year.$ 0

7750 MISCELLANEOUS GENERAL OPERATING is for items not covered in other sections of the budget and to help cover unexpected expenses in other areas.
Total Misc. General Operating Expenses: $
Total Other Expenses: $
TOTAL EXPENSES: $

5800 Reserves
Retained for this year $4,000. Remaining from prior years is 30,000. This reserve fund is vital to the future economic stability of Happiness Condominium Association. These funds are accumulated to repair roofs, roads, tennis courts and to replace equipment, etc. as there useful life ends. Happiness condominium Association has a well-planned, adequately funded replacement/reserve program that will provide sufficient resources to make future repairs when necessary.

Insurance

Before I even start with insurance let me make a suggestion, ask your Insurance broker to attend a board meeting This is very helpful, it puts everyone on the same page so to speak. Your broker is (hopefully) experienced with condominium insurance and should be happy to attend and answer all your questions. Having a rapport with the broker is important. If you have a question the manager or a designated board member(usually the president) can call and get a first hand answer from an expert. Going to an expert is my recommendation with whatever the question and don't forget the manager's opinion. We will talk about the manager in a short while.

It takes many years to understand fully all the exposures and risks that an association or for that matter any business has. The insurance industry has had much experience with condominiums and has for the most part developed standard "ALL RISK" policies for them. Sometimes also referred to as (SMP) special multi peril policies . They are very familiar with the needs of homeowner associations and they have developed these packages just for them. There is a standard policy with most insurance companies. We will not get into bidding for insurance for that is a bit more advanced but it is important that your broker have a copy of the documents to be sure the limits are at least as much as required and I say again, at a least as required. Please remember no matter what the size of your community, proper insurance is extremely important. Any losses that are not covered can have a devastating effect on the community as a whole. It is your responsibility to protect the soundness of the community to the best of your ability and guard against unbudgeted losses or the need for special assessments. Therefore you must protect against potential losses. **The BOD is ultimately responsible to make sure that the association is properly insured against insurable losses.** Certainly insured at the minimum of the documents requirements, that is without exception but have input from other professionals and document that in the minutes. Document your discussion and the reasoning behind your decision. The condominium association maintains insurance on the common elements but the homeowner on the interior of for their unit, as well as those areas designated as owned individually by him or her in the governing documents. Most mortgage companies require proof of coverage from the associations insurance carrier a "certificate of insurance" before settlement indicating that the association is adequately insured and what the limits of coverage are. There are four (4) points that should be considered when considering the types and amounts of insurance coverage for your community:

1. Review the legal documents of your community (you know that's my biggy)
2. Check current relevant state, local or federal requirements and make sure the documents are in fact minimum guidelines.
3. Make sound business judgement, to do this you need to get as much information from professionals as possible, insurance brokers and your manager.
4. This is the step sometimes forgotten, check with the various lending institutions like FHA, VA, FMNA and be sure your limits meet with there requirements. You want to be sure that any homeowner can purchase in your community so check with their organizations to be sure.

Types of coverage…Property Insurance: This insurance provides for coverage on all the buildings and structure, that is structure of the buildings and protects the association against loss or damage by fire or other such acts that involves the common areas and common buildings. If your community has condominium ownership to which most commonly is responsible for the exterior of the entire bldg. this will be covered as common Elements. If it is fee simple ownership and the documents indicate the individual owner is responsible for the roofing, siding and exterior of the building then it must be included in their homeowner policy since it is not common property.

Common Elements include equipment and contents i.e. club-house or maintenance shop.. as well as any personal property OWNED AND MAINTAINED BY THE ASSOCIATION...you must understand and so must the owners, the distinction between the covered property that is commonly owned and maintained and that belonging to the individual homeowner. I don't want to get that technical, so this is an area to discuss with your insurance broker and I recommend an open meeting of the membership specifically called to help answer owners question on this subject. Be sure to check the documents for a "common elements" clear definition.

With condominium ownership generally the common area extends into the building to the common electric and pipes, within the walls and exterior of the building itself.. meaning the common pipes used by more then one in a building are owned and maintained by the association as a whole.i.e. the building has a common sewer line for instance and the sewer backs up affecting more than one unit, that is the system within the building that is maintained and owned in common by the association. IT AFFECTS MORE THAN ONE UNIT it is therefore "common" plumbing. Included as association property is all recreational facilities, tennis courts, pool, and clubhouse...Good tip for you,. when going through the process of reviewing and comparing insurance policies with the broker be sure to ask for what is called the "BEST" rating. A guide

for the insurance industry rating the insurance companies for payment of claims. Triple AAA rating is the best. Another hint is to
play a bit with the deductible you might find a substantial differ-
ence in the premiums if you have no deductible versus $1000.00
deductible. Insurance is very expensive so this may be an alternative for you. You should get a bid with a deductible of $500 and
then one at $ 1000 then compare before making a decision. I do
recommend an "all risk policy," this covers the association against
all perils as long as they are not specifically named as excluded.
Typically excluded are, flood, earthquake, termite damage, glass
damage on the clubhouse for instance..but you can have most of
the items included on separate policies if they are important to the
board and your specific community and location.

Ok, now the liability coverage, the COMPREHENSIVE
GENERAL LIABILITY POLICY is the most complete liability
package available. It provides coverage for BODILY
INJURY...PROPERTY DAMAGE...AND MEDICAL PAYMENTS.
With BODILY INJURY coverage, it is pretty straight forward, it
covers damages the association must pay "legally" for bodily injury,
illness or death...THE OLD SLIP AND FALL SO TO SPEAK. Since
it is rare that someone ever takes responsibility for their own
action...when someone falls it MUST be someone else's fault! Even if
you are wearing high heels in an ice storm..it must be somebody else's
fault or more like it..I can get some money out of this! Do I sound
bitter or negative about this topic.. well I am. That is why
condominium insurance premiums are so high. Remember anyone
can sue no matter how ridiculous you think the claim! Even if you
know they can't win...even if you know there was no negligence.
Remember attorney fees are high.(an understatement)..the insurance
is there to pay for the defense. Remember anyone can sue and they
will!!! Unfortunately it is frustrating because in most cases the

insurance company will settle because it cost so much for legal defense its not worth it to them to pursue it.

PROPERTY DAMAGE LIABILITY protects against loss stemming from insured legal liability as a result of damage to another's property. Property Insurance covers protection of association property against loss caused by specific perils. ie..fire MEDICAL PAYMENTS is the coverage that pays for medical costs of any "guest"who has an accident in the "common" area i.e. playground or jogging path..this does not apply to owners who have an accident on the common area....

Umbrella liability protection: the general all risk policy is not sufficient enough to provide coverage in the event of a catastrophe, therefore a umbrella policy is recommend. The umbrella policy is usually written in limit's of $1,000,000. This coverage is important to consider. It provides additional protection above the dollar limits of the liability policy for a relatively SMALL premium. Ok, there are other types of coverage you may want to consider...HOST LIQUOR LIABILITY..if you throw parties at the clubhouse or around the pool and liquor is served, you will be liable in the event someone from the party leaves and wraps his or her car around a tree on the way home. Talk to your insurance professional and manager about this topic if you ever serve or charge for alcoholic beverages at any function on the common area of the property. Now I know this host liquor law doesn't sound kosher to you but it is true. CONTRACTUAL LIABILITY is coverage to protect the association where it is agreed that you will hold harmless another party who has been contracted to work on the common ground. i.e. lawn service, pool service, roofer, siding repair, painter. This coverage must be specifically included in the policy should you wish to include it. Another important tip...you should inform your insurance broker that you will require that any independent contractor doing work for the association will be required to provide a "certificate of insurance" naming your association as "additional insured" for that period. In most instances there is no charge to the contractor for their insurance carrier to provide a certificate of insurance, this is done routinely. That takes some of the burden off the association for contractor liability. Preferably you must find out when a bid or proposal is submitted and certainly before the contract is signed, whether they HAVE insurance. You may find that a contractor bidding on the same job is significantly less in price then another, sometimes it is because the contractor is not insured. I do recommend that you contract with independent contractors that are fully insured. Then you can file their certificate of insurance for safe keeping.

Let's talk a bit about DIRECTORS AND OFFICERS INSURANCE, or what is commonly referred to as D&O insurance coverage. Directors and officers could be personally liable to the association, its members or third parties for what is referred to as "errors and omissions" in the performance of their duties. D&O insurance is needed when the consequences of the board's alleged negligence is a result of mismanagement of the common funds or policies. An example..the board fails to collect delinquent assessments and loses a large sum of money because of a failure to put a lien on that property. Another example of failure to act is when a homeowner claims that the board failed to act and that failure was a direct relation to him or her not being able to sell their unit. Cars on common area, junk piled on the patio, common ground not kept in a reasonable condition. An Association owes that protection against personal liability to it's officers and Directors in the case involving unintentional wrong doing. A person who volunteers his or her services to his neighbors should not be asked to risk substantial personal liability. TIP: **You want to be sure that coverage is extended to the members of all committees who are not Board members as well.** The important aspect of this insurance is that not only coverage for loss or damages which might be awarded but the cost of the defense on any claim or law suit which alleges a D&O liability.

Now the biggy…what acts are NOT covered?..obviously intentional wrongdoing. Typical wrong doings..libel and slander, civil rights violations, illegal acts, fraudulent acts. **Anything ILLEGAL, IMMORAL OR UNETHICAL.** That is why I keep saying that you need to document everything. Attached all pertinent review items to your minutes. Your minutes books should also contain some excepts of the motion indicating some of the discussion that brought you to the decision at hand. Whatever they might be. A tip,..**if a board member is involved emotionally with a subject they should abstain from the final vote.** Remember be fair, listen to all sides and act in the best interest of the community as a whole.

FIDELITY BOND COVERAGE…this coverage protects the association from dishonest employees that have access to the associations funds. Most documents require fidelity bonds. It is recommended that you maintain this coverage regardless of whether it is required in the documents or not. The bond will reimburse the association for any loss it incurs up to the amount of the bond. I would discuss this with the manager and insurance broker as well as reviewing the documents before coming up with an amount of coverage. It is generally affected by your current operating budget. The rule of thumb is that it should be based on at least 3 months income of the operating budget or the reserve fund if anyone has independent access of it.

A bit about transitions.

That is the transitions of control from the developer to the unit owners. Normally in the POS(Public Offering statement) it specifies at what point unit owners get involved in the community. Typically at points like 25% owned there may be one spot on the board for a unit owner. Remember the developer wants the majority vote until he is through. Then it may be at 50% when another unit owner gets on the board and then 75% involvement, at which time the owners may in fact have the majority vote on the board.

The most important aspect about the transition is to have a good relationship with the developer. You don't want to seem as though you think he or she is trying to rip the community off. The transition of property needs to be handled most gingerly and is very important because it could potentially cost the association a lot of money, either to correct an area or to litigate.

When a developer is going to build the community he goes to the township or city and presents his plan. To be sure the builder is going to finish the project and adhere to the stipulations the planning board has made, they take money as a bond. This bond is twp. insurance so to speak, that the work will be completed.

When an area is complete the builder will go to that entity for inspection to get there bond (money) back. The bond is often quite substantial. Of course to mean anything it must be. The planning board and engineers may have requested some things to the builder in order to get an approval initially. Usually landscaping demands, plantings, french drains etc. That is why you see so many dead trees when the developer is gone. In order to get the bond money back the developer plants the requested trees in a certain area in 95 degree temperature in july and of course they comply at the time but in late September all the trees are dead. In that case usually the builder will fess up and replant but his happens all the time. You would think the twp. would be wise to it and make some adjustments but for the most part they don't. That is why I stress having a good relationship with the builder. Of course if the builder has a bad reputation and does not want any impute of that type you may be out of luck.

It is so important as the community becomes more involved on the board that a transition committee/procedure be formulated. Asking the developer to notify the committee when specific areas are going to be evaluated by the city or township. You might be able to get the township officials to let you know when they will be inspecting so a representative may be present. You are also trying to have a good relationship with the township. The construction supervisor will be a great help if you can work together. Working together is your best hope.

Typically the Association becomes aware that the developer has turned over a part of the community when you complain about a specific problem. It could be a leaking community room or improper drainage in the landscaping, noticing shoddy workmanship on many skylights or leaky windows. At that point you immediately want to know who approved this and why weren't we notified? Isn't our input required by the township.? NO!

The builder doesn't want anything to hold up the money or cost him a penny more. It is however better in the long run for the builder to have a committee (of unit owners)review the requested area for bond release now as opposed to being sued later. It is also better for the association to have a good relationship with the builder and twp.. officials. so as to avoid the kinds of calls that come from not understanding how they could have approved a specific area since it is so obvious that it is flawed. Even with a transition committee some things do change as time goes on and what was approved at the time may not weather well. No one can be sure that there will be no damage or flaws in the future. I still recommend strongly that you try to have the builder work with and approve a transition committee. Suing the builder costs a great deal of money. Even if the correction is made by the builder the costs to the association is an extraordinary amount of time and money to litigate.

I stress then that you slowly begin to have a good relationship with the builder and the twp. and try to get involved with the transition process NOW so you will not be surprised in the end.

A Brief Summary

Let us recap ..we have covered: 1. Glossary 2. Governing documents. 3. Planning a meeting 4. The meeting process 5. Board Burn out test. 6. Architectural application 7. Committee interest form 8. Nominee for the BOD 9. Define committees 10. Revitalizing apathetic communities. 11. Getting volunteers 12. Motions 13. Collection procedures 14. Budget narrative and 15. Evaluation of Management company 16. Insurance.

We covered the public offering statement (POS)containing the governing documents of an association, board meetings and how to have the meetings run more efficiently and effectively. We covered open meetings, revitalizing your community, trying to pool all its resources and ways to get more participation from the membership. We dealt with more effective communication, the need for committees, structure and guidelines for them, architectural controls and the need to make sure the community is aware of all the rules and regulations as well as how to present applications for modification, making sure the process is done in a timely way. We had some advice for board members, the need for rules and there enforcement, working with the local government to help with violation enforcement. Had sample collection procedures and budgets with easier to understand (user friendly as they say) narratives explaining what is included in each line item. Covered insurance needs that protect the community as a whole as well as the directors and officers that are responsible for it.

That's a lot of ground we covered…now at this point I would like to end in an area that is near and dear to my heart.. your relationship with the manager or managing agent .

Working with the Manager or Management Agent

This is a very important point that I want to convey to all of you…all of the things I conveyed are not meant to direct you to stand over the manager or management company and get involved in the day to day work or to do the work yourself. The board should not be involved in the day to day operations. I repeat, the board should not be involved in the day to day operations of the association. This course is designed to give you the tools you need to be more effective in your role or potential role on the board of directors. I am teaching this course because I feel such a tremendous feeling of satisfaction that you can take these tools and use them to better the quality of life in your community. Your knowledge gained from this course is not taught so that your comments and questions to the manager or managing agent would intimidate…but rather use to work together to be sure the community association is working effectively and efficiently. Remember this is not your actual profession but it is for the manager. Although you are protecting your investment and making your home a better place to live.. property management is not your specially. You need to trust your manager.

You need someone in that position who is protecting the association and its interests at all times. Someone who can advise you and guide and help in your decision making process. Someone who can advise and assist the board with their knowledge and experience and one who can articulate well to both you and to the community. One that can maintain a rapport with the local government for their help, as we discussed they have a role in enforcement of rules. Stay with me on this a moment ..suppose at your job you had a real estate manager who suddenly had financial interest in your job or business and he or she begins to tell you what is best for your office or store. They would need much knowledge and experience in order to give some sound advise to you. You need to understand the same. Ask the questions, let the manager know what your concerns are, your comments, your suggestions, be specific, let he or she explain the history of a situation or what their experience has been with that situation. Get all the facts.. not just hearsay. but all the facts before you come to a conclusion. Treat the manager as you would want to be treated on your job. Good manager's are hard to find. They can make your life a whole lot easier…and continuity is important in communities.

So be respectful and hopefully you will get that in return. Be aware of the chain of command. Talk to your manager and if there is a problem with someone else on the staff…let them handle the problem. If you think the manager should be doing something else or something different then they are..discuss it with them…**don't just gripe about it!** Make sure you understand each other. Tell them what the Board expects. Good communication with the manager is essential to the success of a community. Treat the manager the way you would want to be treated by a superior at your place of employment. If you have a management company talk with your company representative or regional manager and explain what you expect or what you are not getting from the manager. Put that in writing and make sure you are protected and that you have crossed your T's and dotted all your I's before a dismissal is made or recommendation for a change of manager or management company.

OK. Some things I feel that you need as a board member…above all be sure you have the (POS) public offering statement containing all the documents. This is a must! Make sure you have the minutes and any pertinent information along with those minutes. Make sure you have a list of any additional rules, architectural guidelines or amendments since the board has taken control from the developer. Find out how the rules and guidelines were distributed to all the members including absentee owners.

As a board member you should have a list of any current committees, regular or ad hoc (one time)and the names of the members of those committees along with their meeting schedule, of course you want a meeting schedule for the BOD meetings and ask how owners are notified and where is the meeting schedule posted? Is the whole year of meeting dates listed and given to the membership. When is the agenda and meeting packet for board meetings given to the current board members. Who handles the agenda should you need to include an item. You should have a current budget, monthly statements, minutes for a minimum of two years, the last two audits, emergency telephone numbers for on- call staff including the manager, telephone numbers of all the other board members including information on how long they have served. It is a good idea to ask the manager for a one on one orientation meeting between the two of you, to discuss some of the topics that you may have questions on and to get to know the manager and his or her concerns. You will get an idea also of their knowledge and experience. Of course now that you are armed with information from this course ..you can ask the manager for the information given to owners and any rules booklets to see if the changes are up to date, collection procedures and discuss insurance issues with the manager as well as any ideas for revitalizing the community, newsletters, welcoming committees, parties etc.

If a management company is contracted get a copy of the contract and see the list of duties they are responsible for. The role and duties of the management agent is specified in the contract. You may think the management company is not responsive enough because they only come onto the property once a week, well that may be specified in the contract, more on site attention cost more money...so check out the contract before you jump. For a smooth flow of operation, there should be ONE contact person from the board who the manager talks with through the month. This eliminates 5 or 7 calls to or from the manager about the same thing. One call and then he or she can get to solving the problem, that is much quicker. Usually the contact person is the president of the Board.

I have to say that I feel that community members who have enrolled in this course will be the most successful, effective board members in their community. Not just because of the tools received in this course but also because you felt it was important enough to take the time to know more. Good luck to you in all your future endeavors.

Glossary

Actual cash value. Amount of money that would be required to repair or replace existing building or improvement with another of like kind in the same condition, thereby taking into account depreciation; replacement cost less depreciation.

Additional living expense insurance. Coverage that would reimburse the insured for living costs in excess of normal living expenses if loss of or damage to property forced the insured to maintain temporary residence elsewhere.

Ad hoc committee. Special committee appointed to carry out a specific nonrecurring task and disbanded when that task is completed.

Administrative expenses. Cost of goods or services that can be attributed to the management of affairs of a condominium.

Agenda. Sequence in which issues are to be taken up in a meeting.

Agent. One who has the authority to act for or represent another; see Insurance agent, Management agent.

Agreed amount insurance. Policy under which coinsurance clause is waived if insured carries insurance of an agreed amount and under which insurer agrees to pay face amount on the policy in the event of total loss of property covered or upon occurrence of a stated contingency.

All-risk insurance. Policy under which a loss resulting from any cause other than those causes specifically excluded by name is considered to be covered.

Amend. Modify or change; under parliamentary procedure, modify a motion by adding, deleting, or substituting words.

Amendment. Revision of a governing document or, under parliamentary procedure, a motion.

Amenity. Facility that is part of common areas and increases physical comfort, such as a swimming pool or tennis court.

Amenity rental fee. Fixed charge paid by unit owner or guest for use of common facility and/or limited common area.

Annual membership meeting. Once-a-year assemblage of unit owners required by governing documents to conduct association business, such as electing a board of directors.

Appraisal. Survey of a property and estimate of its value by an expert in property analysis.

Architectural restrictions. Standards and restrictions that limit what unit owners can do to change the outward appearance of their units and outline procedures unit owners must follow to make changes to the exterior of units.

Articles of incorporation. Formal document that, when filed, sets up an association as a corporation under the laws of the applicable state.

Assembly. Group of persons gathered for some common purpose.

Assessment. Amount charged against each unit owner, based on percentages of budgeted common expenses, to fund the developer.

Adjusted basis Original cost or book value of an asset for income tax purposes, administration, maintenance, and management of a condominium.

Association insurance policy. Written contract combining liability and property protection into one package and designed to cover common areas of a condominium, usually including the structure, and take precedence over unit owners' policies; also called master insurance policy.

Audit. Examination of financial records and accounts to verify their accuracy and determine if financial statements adequately reflect an association's financial status.

Balance sheet. Financial statement that indicates the financial status of an association at a specific time by listing its assets, liabilities, and members' equity.

Ballot. Paper used to cast secret vote. Basis See Adjusted basis.

Best's Key Rating Guide: Property-Casualty An annually issued guide featuring comprehensive statistics on the financial condition, general standing, and transactions of property and casualty insurance companies throughout the United States.

Blanket fidelity bond. Contract covering loss of association money or real or personal property when such a loss is due to dishonesty of an employee.

Board of Directors. (BOD.) Official governing body of a condominium association elected by members of the association; also called board of managers or board of trustees.

Building Officials and Code Administrators International, Inc. (BOCA.) A nonprofit organization that set up a model building code used widely in United States municipalities.

Bylaws. Secondary laws of an association that govern its internal affairs and deal with routine operational and administrative matters; also called code of regulations.

Condominium unit. That part of a condominium development, probably a space of air or three-dimensional area located within the walls, floor, and ceiling of a condominium structure, privately owned and independently and exclusively used by a unit owner.

Contingency reserves. Funds set aside to cover unanticipated emergencies or major expenditures not included in the current fiscal year operating budget.

Conversion. Transfer of multifamily rental development to condominium form of ownership through sale of individual living units; multifamily dwelling whose ownership has been so transferred.

Cooperative. Corporation that holds real estate, specifically a multifamily dwelling, shareholders in which have the right to live in one of its units; also called a co-op.

Declaration. Legal document that, when filed, commits land to condominium use, creates a condominium association and serves as its constitutional law, physically describes a condominium, defines the method of determining each unit owner's share of the common areas, and outlines responsibilities and restrictions; also called declaration of codes, covenants, and restrictions or master deed.

Deductible. Specific amount to be subtracted from a loss and written into an insurance policy as a means of effecting a decrease in premium.

Default. Failure to fulfill or live up to terms of an agreement.

Deferred maintenance. Upkeep that may be scheduled at a future date without allowing a minor problem to become a major one.

Delinquency. Overdue assessment payment.

Depreciation. Decrease in value of property because of physical deterioration resulting from wear and tear, functional inability to serve its use as well as a new property designed for the same purpose, or location obsolescence resulting from external and environmental factors.

Directors' and officers' liability insurance. Protection against loss arising out of alleged errors in judgment, breaches of duty, and wrongful acts of a board of directors and/or officers in carrying out their prescribed duties.

Easement. Right to use land owned by someone else for certain limited purposes, such as for party driveways, drainage, etc.

Emergency maintenance. Necessary repairs that cannot be predicted and require immediate attention.

Endorsement/amendments. Attachment to an insurance policy that in some way modifies its coverage.

Errors and omissions insurance. Protection against loss arising out of an alleged error or oversight on the part of an insured professional while performing prescribed duties.

Escrow. Agreement that something, usually money, given to a third party be held until certain conditions are met.

Extended coverage insurance. Policy that extends basic fire policy to cover property loss caused by additional perils, usually including windstorm, hail, explosion, riot and civil commotion, aircraft, vehicles, and smoke.

Fee simple. Absolute interest. Most complete type of private ownership of real estate which gives title holder the right to possess, control, use, and dispose of it at will.

Federal Home Loan Mortgage Corporation (FHLMC.) A private corporation authorized by Congress to purchase mortgages from savings and loan institutions; also known as Freddie Mac.

Federal Housing Authority (FHA.) Federal agency that functions as an insurer of mortgage loans.

Federal National Mortgage Association (FNMA.) A privately-owned, for-profit organization created by Congress that purchases and sells residential mortgages; also known as Fannie Mae.

Fidelity bond. Formal agreement under which an employer would be reimbursed for loss, up to an amount specified, that may result from a dishonest act of covered employee occupying a position of trust.

Fiduciary relationship. Agreement based on trust in which one person or group of persons handles financial transactions for another or others.

Financial statement. Report that indicates certain information concerning financial position of an association.

Fiscal controls. Procedures for regulating and verifying financial activities.

Fiscal year. Twelve-month period for which an association plans use of funds.

Fixed expenses. Costs that remain relatively stable.

Fixture. Item of personal property that is annexed, attached, or affixed to or installed in real property, such as plumbing fixtures or wall-to-wall carpeting.

Fraud. Deliberate deception practiced to secure unlawful gain.

Full agency management. A plan for handling all or designated aspects of the affairs of an association whereby a property management firm and/or its agent are contracted to perform a full range of administrative, maintenance, and operational tasks for an association.

Garden condominium. Multifamily dwelling under condominium ownership that usually is no more than three stories tall, has units arranged horizontally and vertically, and is built around a courtyard; also called low-rise condominium.

Governing documents. Set of legal papers, filed by a developer with the appropriate local government office, that submit land to condominium use and create and govern a condominium association.

Heating, ventilation, air-conditioning system (HVAC.) The unit regulating the even distribution of heat and fresh air throughout a building.

High-rise condominium. Multifamily dwelling under condominium ownership that utilizes an arrangement of units placed one on top of the other.

Hold harmless clause. Contractual provision that shifts liability inherent in a situation to another party; see Indemnification.

Homeowners association (HOA.) An organization of homeowners having individual lots as part of a development whose major purpose is to maintain and provide for the rights of owners to have easement in the use of common areas.

Host liquor liability insurance. Protection against loss arising out of insured's legal responsibility as a result of an accident attributed to the use of liquor dispensed but not sold by an association and/or used in common areas.

House rules and regulations Guidelines related to day-to-day conduct in common areas and relationships between unit owners.

Indemnification. Condition, usually contractual, of being protected against possible damage, loss, or suit; see Hold harm-less clause.

Judgment. Court decree of indebtedness to another and amount of that indebtedness.

Liability insurance. Coverage for damages arising out of insured's legal responsibility and resulting from injuries to other persons or damage to their property.

Lien. Claim or attachment, enforceable at law, to have a debt or other charge satisfied out of a person's property.

Limited common areas. Property that physically is part of a condominium's common areas but is reserved for the exclusive use of a particular unit owner or group of unit owners.

Line item. Budget Format listing of expenses by category.

Loss assessment insurance. Unit owner protection that would cover special assessments the owner may be obligated to pay because a loss incurred by the association was not otherwise adequately insured.

Management agent. Representatives of a management firm.

Master association. Organization of unit owners of more than one condominium created to maintain, operate, manage, and finance recreational facilities of which they share the use; also called common association or umbrella association.

Medical payments insurance. Coverage that voluntarily provides for payment of medical and similar expenses of persons injured in common areas regardless of the question of fault or legal liability.

Metes and bounds. Legal description of real property in which boundaries are defined by directions and distances.

Minutes. Official record of proceedings of a meeting.

Motion. Formal proposal put before an assembly on which action must be taken.

Mulch. Protective covering, usually organic, placed around plants to protect against weed growth and help soil retain moisture.

Occupancy restrictions. Limitations on who may and may not buy and/or live in condominium units.

On-site management. Plan for managing a condominium association whereby a person is hired and works exclusively for the association and handles all or designated aspects of its affairs.

Operating expenses. Costs incurred to maintain a property and keep it productive of services.

Operating reserves. Funds set aside for the payment of an annual expense.

Organization meeting. First meeting of an association at which directors are elected.

Ownership interest. Legal share, expressed in percentages, each unit owner has in common areas.

Parliamentary procedure. Established rules of parliamentary law and unwritten rules of courtesy "Robert's rules of order" used to facilitate the transaction of business in deliberative assemblies.

Payroll expenses. Costs of wages, vacation and sick pay, holiday pay, group medical benefits, and employee benefits.

Personal injury liability insurance. Protection against loss arising out of personal insults, such as slander, liable, or false arrest, allegedly delivered by the insured.

Personal property. Possessions that are temporary or movable, as opposed to real property which is fixed; personality.

Planned unit development (PUD.) A form of development that usually includes a mixture of open space, single-family homes, townhouses, condominiums or cooperatives, rental units, and recreational and commercial facilities within a defined area and specifically zoned arrangement.

Plat Survey plan or map and descriptions of a tract of land showing property lines, easements, etc.

Point of order. Demand that chair enforce parliamentary rules which are being violated.

Public offering statement (POS.) Contains the governing documents of the association. The declaration, bylaws and deeds.

Preventive maintenance. Program of inspection and regular care that allows potential problems to be detected and solved early or prevented altogether.

Property damage liability insurance. Protection against loss arising out of insured's legal responsibility as a result of damage to or destruction of another's property.

Property insurance. Protection of insured's real or personal property against loss or damage caused by specified perils.

Property tax. Fee levied by local governments against real estate, business equipment, and inventories.

Prorate. Divide, distribute, or assess in proportionate shares.

Proxy. Authorization given to one person to vote in place of another.

Quorum. Minimum number of members that must be present or votes that must be represented in person or by proxy at a meeting in order for

Recording secretary. An assistant to the secretary of the board of directors who takes the minutes at a board meeting.

Replacement cost. Amount of money required to repair and replace an existing property with property of the same material and construction without deducting for depreciation.

Replacement reserves. Funds set aside for probable repair and replacement of common area components at some future time.

Rescind. Cancel or nullify a previous action by an assembly.

Reserves. Funds set aside for special purposes, specifically, to enable an association to meet nonrecurring and/or major expenses.

Robert's Rules of Order. Recognized formal guidelines for conducting a business meeting.

Self-management. Plan of running a condominium whereby unit owners carry out policy decisions of and handle affairs for an association.

Service contract. Formal agreement that certain work necessary for the continuing operation of a condominium be performed in exchange for specified compensation.

Special assessment. Fee levied against unit owners to cover unexpected expenses.

Special meeting. Unscheduled meeting called by board or membership to discuss urgent business.

Standing committee. Group of people formed to handle ongoing business on a certain subject.

Subcommittee. Subordinate committee composed of members appointed from a main committee to handle a specified task within the main committee's responsibilities.

Subrogation. Legal process of substitution by which an insurance company seeks from a third party, who may have caused a loss, recovery of the amount paid to the policyholder.

Tort action. Legal filing of civil suit arising out of a wrongful act, damages, or injury involving liability.

Townhouse condominium. Multifamily dwelling under condominium ownership that utilizes an arrangement of units attached side by side, often rowhouses with individual entrances; also called zero lot line houses.

Umbrella liability insurance. Protection against losses in excess of amounts covered by other liability insurance policies.

Underwriter. Employee of insurance company who reviews applications for coverage, decides if it should be given, and determines appropriate rates.

Undivided interest. Ownership that is inseparable and cannot be divided or severed, such as a condominium unit and its share of common areas.

Unit deed. Legal instrument that, when filed, transfers title of a condominium unit and its undivided portion of common areas from one owner to another.

Unit owner insurance. policy specifically designed to provide property and liability coverage to meet needs of owners of condominium units.

Use restrictions. Rules and regulations, often prohibitive in nature, that regulate human behavior in common areas and between neighbors.

Waiver. Surrender of a right or privilege.

Water damage insurance. Protection against property loss caused by water, with certain exceptions.

Committee Interest Form

DATE:
NAME:
ADDRESS:
TELEPHONE:　　　Home　　　　　　Business

I would like to work on the following committee (Please circle number in order of preference):

1. MAINTENANCE COMMITTEE (Exterior & Grounds)
2. BUDGET AND FINANCE COMMITTEE
3. ARCHITECHUAL & DESIGN REVIEW COMMITTEE
4. RULES AND REGULATIONS COMMITTEE
5. SOCIAL/RECREATION COMMITTEE
6. NEWSLETTER COMMITTEE
7. WELCOMING COMMITTEE
8. INSURANCE COMMITTEE
9. NOMINATING COMMITTEE
10. TRANSITION/ACCEPTANCE COMMITTEE

I am volunteering for:_____At this time. I have a (considerable) (moderate) (small) amount of time to devote.

The most convenient time for me is (weekends) (days) (evenings) (whenever needed).

Nominee for Board of Directors

Name:_____

Address:_____

YEARS OF RESIDENCY IN OUR COMMUNITY_____

1. ANY PERSONAL:INFORMATION YOU WISH TO SHARE:_____
_____

2.EMPLOYMENT_____
_____

    Number Years._____

    Brief Job Description:_____

    Position:_____

3.EDUCATION: High School:_____

    College:_____

    Major:_____

    Minor:_____

    Other:_____

4. ASSOCIATION COMMITTEE INVOLVEMENT:_____
_____

5. OTHER PROFESSIONAL, CIVIC, OR SPECIAL INTEREST COM-
MITTEE OR GROUP INVOLVEMENT:_____
_____
_____

ANY COMMENTS:

_____

_____

_____

_____

Are You Burntout?

Answer Yes OR No

1. Do you find it difficult to fall asleep at night, even though you feel tired much of the time?
2. Do you often fall asleep at Board meetings?
3. Is your blood pressure too high, or does your back ache or is your stomach chronically upset?
4. Have you given up hope that anyone will ever show appreciation for the work you are doing?
5. Are your concerns about association business interfering with your "paying" job?
6. Are you solving the problems of the homeowners but letting your marriage fall apart?
7. Do you often feel that the homeowners are out to get you?
8. Do you believe you better get them, before they get you?
9. Have you gotten an unlisted phone number?
10. When a homeowner greets you in the lobby, dc) you question his ulterior motive?
11. If you make a mistake, do you usually find someone else to blame?
12. Are open meetings a source of anxiety and stress for you?
13. Do you frequently "tune out" what other people are saying?
14. If your ideas are challenged, do you "lose your cool"?
15. Have you developed an "l don't give a damn" attitude?

16. Do you spend most of your time at social functions discussing association business?
17. Do you try to avoid social functions out of fear that homeowners may seize the opportunity to make complaints?
18. Do you envy less involved homeowners their free time?
19. Are you convinced that you are the only board member doing any work?
20. Do you often wonder whatever made you run for the board in the first place?

TOTAL: Yes   No

If your yes's out number your no's, then you may be experiencing burnout. Those who resist burnout may have internalized their need for approval to such an extent that they do not depend on Feedback from the homeowners. It really comes as a shock when they realize that the homeowners don't share their confidence in their work. Others may be able to shield themselves against burnout by creating a dictatorship. If they tolerate no opposition and if their decisions go unchallenged, then they may remain on the board indefinitely. The system works best when the homeowners don't care what the board does as long as it doesn't raise the maintenance charges. In this instance, it isn't the board that is burned out; it is the community.

Others who resist burnout have come on the board with so much enthusiasm and so many good Intention's that it simply takes burnout a little longer to surface. These board members really care whether the homeowners approve of what they do, and they do their best to make everybody happy. Sooner or later, they learn they cannot please everyone.

Evaluation of Management Firm

Name of firm_____

1. General appearance of their office.

2. General employee attitude.

3. How are phone calls are handled.

4. Office equipment: up to date; operating condition, etc.

5. Clerical capabilities: general correspondence, newsletter, etc.

6. Firm's philosophy of community association management.

7. Years of experience managing community associations.

8. Bookkeeping and financial systems.

9. Samples of all standard delinquency correspondence.

10. Technical knowledge of association management and maintenance.

11. Approach to handling rules and regulations enforcement.

12. Sample of letters for violations of the rules and regulations.

13. How do they handle after-hour/emergency calls.

14. Understanding of governing documents.

15. Approach to obtaining association homeowner involvement.

16. Frequency of property inspections.

17. Approach to communicating with residents

18. Management of nearby associations. Obtain list of clients and speak with them.

19. Philosophy of communications with Board and its committees.

20. Total Number of associations managed.

21. Client turnover.

22. After meeting with the BOD your overall impression of manager that will be assigned to the association.

23. Management Fee. $

24. Additional Charges: $
   A. Transfer Process $
   B. Lien Filing $
   C. Mailing of Registered Letters $
   D. Court Time per Hour $
   E. Mailing of Newsletter $
   F. Mailing of notices $
   F. Photocopying $
   G. Meeting attendance $
   H. Additional on-site meetings $
   I. Misc. time/charges $

25. Rating by other current clients:
   A.

   B.

   C.

   D.

Made in the USA
Middletown, DE
09 January 2018